INmotion
COUNSELING

....

In Motion Counseling is a church-based recovery ministry,
which began in the Denver Church of Christ in 2011.
Disciples In Motion and Grief Journey In Motion groups
are now operating in many ICOC churches.
For more information, go to: **www.inmotioncounseling.org**

....

*I dedicate this book in loving memory to Lt. Col. Earl B. Sumerlin Jr.
and Catherine Elizabeth Sumerlin, my beloved parents.
My dad modeled honor and my mom taught me a love
of education. Their love was without boundaries.*

The Lord is close to the brokenhearted and saves those who are crushed in spirit.
—Psalm 34:18

Grief is a club no one chooses to join and the dues are always more than anyone wants to pay. Our family's involuntary induction to this club left our heads whirling, our hearts broken and our spirits crushed—the long walk through the valley of the shadow of death. I will forever remember the words of our son Michael when our youngest son David died at age 36: "I didn't realize that brokenhearted meant your heart actually broke."

Marcia and I lost all four of our parents, my sister, our son, a sister-in-law and several aunts and uncles in the last few years. We were blessed to be caretakers for some. Reaching out for God through these valleys, it dawned on me that this is the largest club on earth and its membership will only grow. I knew it intellectually but it was like a mysterious, secret society until I was forced to join.

When I look back at my response to others in this club, I shudder to think of some of the ways I tried to comfort them as an outsider. Even good-hearted disciples of Jesus and the most well intentioned, loving people can say unbelievable things. How can you know, until you have been there? Job's friends have been around for a long time.

The tremendous global outpouring of love to our family provided me with what feels like a graduate degree in how to mourn with those who mourn. Engaging in grief classes, in private conversations with dear friends and strangers and bonding deeply to our loved ones makes that walk bearable.

But there is one great answer and reason for all of that. God is the Father of all comfort. He works through or in spite of every single person and circumstance. He invited me in to ask any question, express every emotion, share every doubt and fear. He is the only One who can handle it all.

I have come to these conclusions:

1. God did not intend for us to experience death. He put man and woman in Paradise where they would live forever. When they were enticed and chose to sin, the cost was a hard life and death. (Genesis 3) Godhas grieved the hurt and loss of every one of his billions of children for thousands of years. Yet He was willing for his One and Only Son to die, be raised from the dead and free us from our sin and death (1 Corinthians 15).

THE GRIEF JOURNEY:

Finding Peace in All of Life's Losses

Dr. Timothy Sumerlin

The Grief Journey: Finding Peace in All of Life's Losses
Second Edition. Copyright @ 2018 by Dr. Timothy Sumerlin
ISBN: 978-1-941988-49-7

Printed in the United States of America.

All Scripture references are from the Holy Bible, New International Version, copyright 1973, 1978, 1984 by the International Bible Society. Used by permission of Zondervan Bible Publishers.

Scripture taken from the NEW AMERICAN STANDARD BIBLE(R), Copyright (C) 1960,1962,1963,1968,1971,1972,1973,1975,1977,1995 by The Lockman Foundation. Used by permission.

Cover design: Roy Applesamy. Interior design: Laura Witt.

Published by Illumination Publishers,
6010 Pinecreek Ridge Court, Spring, Texas 77379.
Additional copies available at www.ipibooks.com

2. God wants people to accompany us through the valley. He knows we cannot do it on our own. We need to let them walk with us.

3. Too few churches have groups for mourning with those who mourn.

Dr. Timothy Sumerlin is one of those people. He has been a constant source of encouragement and a listening ear for me the last two years particularly. Tim's vulnerability in this book helps you understand his grief journey not just as a professional counselor, but as a disciple, husband, father, son, and friend. He has chosen to find God in his grief and to help many others. *The Grief Journey: Finding Peace in All of Life's Losses* is Tim's giving back what God has given him.

This series will help you individually and in a group setting. You have a new friend to walk with you through that lonesome valley. You will find it even better if you will invite others to join you. Start a group in your church or in your community.

If you have not yet joined the Grief Club, here is your chance to get an inside view of how to help the hurting and how to prepare for your initiation.

Grief Club membership is lifetime. But we don't have to camp out in the valley of the shadow of death. God longs to show us the way to the other side.

ACKNOWLEDGEMENTS

The grief journey is an intricate, emotionally laden, and often difficult process. Many of us avoid the emotions associated with grief as we encounter these experiences. For me, grief hit me hard in the face, making me confront the process head on. The journey presented challenging, yet rewarding results. *Grief Journey: Finding Peace in All of Life's Losses* was thus born.

Sir Isaac Newton wrote over 300 years ago, "If I have seen further than others, it is by standing on the shoulders of giants." We all learn by standing on the shoulders of giants—those men and women who have gone before us, blazing a trail of knowledge, inspiration, and insight that we learn from and hopefully build on. There are some that I want to acknowledge as having informed and inspired my thinking about grief. I cite these authors throughout the book as warranted.

Russell Friedman and John James wrote an influential piece on grief, *The Grief Recovery Handbook, 20th Anniversary Expanded Edition: The Action Program for Moving Beyond Death, Divorce, and Other Losses including Health, Career, and Faith*[1], which not only taught me, but also ushered me through my own personal grief. Craig Lounsbrough, on his personal journey of his mother's passing, eloquently penned *An Autumn's Journey: Deep Growth in the Grief and Loss of Life's Seasons,* which I found inspirational. Dr. Wolfelt's, *Understanding Your Grief: Ten Essential Touchstones* has added a scholarly touch to my writings and finally, C.S. Lewis' *A Grief Observed*, has brought a loving, yet sometimes mystical God into my grief journey.

I have many courageous friends, including Greg and Theresa Jackson, Chris and Allison Jacobs, Chip and Judy Roberts, and the many who have attended *Grief Journey* groups. Their inspiration, love, vulnerability, and encouragement in both my writing and on my personal journey of grief has been extraordinarily helpful. In particular, I'm indebted to the spring, 2016 Denver church grief group who provided great insight and affirmation for the book. I stand on sacred ground in their presence. Also, thanks to my friend, John Lusk, for encouraging me to write this book after that "perplexing" letter.

Many times, a family is either broken up or drawn together during times of grief. My brothers and sister have provided much comfort and emotional support during the recent losses of our beloved mother and father. My parents' passing and the subsequent family connections, has added a rich layer of love to our family, which I cherish.

Much gratitude to Jim McCraigh and Erica Kim for reviewing my manuscripts. John and Leslie Dowaschinski have provided many hours of editing and textual proficiency. Laura Witt with Hanna Design provided design support—all professionals, extraordinaire. Roger and Marcia Lamb, from *Disciples Today* have provided great encouragement (and the Foreword) and have become friends and models of humbly walking this arduous journey of grief. I feel a deep sense of gratitude to Clay Jackson and Toney Mulhollan, Contributing Editors, for their many hours of editorial contributions for this edition.

Of course, many thanks go to my own family—my wife, Jackie, my daughter, Danielle and her husband, Adrian, and my son, Timothy. Their support has been spectacular over the years and I cannot imagine doing this work without their insights, encouragement, and love.

Unique to this grief book from many others, is the perspective I've developed from the Bible. God, the originator of all life, is also the Expert in the grief journey. He begins life and often watches it fade away in ignominy. God knows loss at every level. He sees his created nature die, his people pass on, and his dreams for those people often die—God knows grief (Genesis 6:6). Yet he is also familiar with grief on a very intimate level—the loss of his Son, Jesus. God modeled for us how to grieve and works to help us journey through grief and come out on the other side, closer to him—God knows.

Soli Deo Gloria!

END NOTE

[1] I was immensely impacted by the concepts found in this book. Easy and simple to apply, they helped me greatly during my grief journey. Russell Friedman and John James pioneered a masterful work in the grief genre: *The Grief Recovery Handbook, 20th Anniversary Expanded Edition: The Action Program for Moving Beyond Death, Divorce, and Other Losses including Health, Career, and Faith,* HarperCollins Publishers, 2009.

BENEFITS

FIVE SUSTAINABLE BENEFITS
FOR *GRIEF JOURNEY* GROUP MEMBERS

Grief Journey: Finding Peace in All of Life's Losses is a book that can be used both in a group setting and individually. Grief and mourning are best worked on with others in a safe, confidential, and loving environment. We encourage your church to provide *Grief Journey* groups at least twice a year (see Appendices B and E). These 8-week groups provide the needed support for church members and visitors to walk this journey together, most effectively.

However, some are either not ready to attend a group or are not in a situation where one is provided. In that case, *Grief Journey* will provide a rich experience for the reader. Below are five sustainable benefits:

1. Many find the resolution to complex grief issues while engaging in *Grief Journey*. Learning to be with Christians who are working through difficult challenges, allows the griever to understand God's grace, mercy, and acceptance in ways not previously understood.

2. Readers connect to God in new and meaningful ways. God's grace, mercy, and vision for a hopeful future is illustrated throughout the book and in the group sessions and are incorporated into a member's grief journey. Many readers find freedom from years of struggle and hardship.

3. Group members learn vulnerability with others in a safe and confidential environment. Many learn how to understand and honor boundaries in their lives. Often, members bring this spirit of openness and vulnerability into their relationships, which allow others to open up and learn vulnerability in a greater way.

4. Valuable grief recovery concepts are learned that may be applied throughout a lifetime. The grief journey is an ongoing process where *Grief Journey* members learn vital life skills.

5. Restored relationships are an important part of the recovery process. *Grief Journey* readers learn the value in reconciling with

loved ones who hurt them during their lifetime. These restored relationships influence many other relationships and even, future generations.

What benefits would you realize by engaging in *Grief Journey?* _____

_____

_____

_____

_____

_____

_____

_____

_____

Introduction: What is Grief Recovery?
Page 11

INTRODUCTION

For no one is cast off
by the Lord forever.
Though he brings grief, he will show compassion,
so great is his unfailing love.
For he does not willingly bring affliction
or grief to anyone.

—Lamentations 3:31-33

In the fall of 2006 I received the most devastating phone call of my life—my mom had lung cancer. What? In my family?! How could this be? She had never smoked a day in her life, was always the picture of health, and we all expected her to live well into her 90s, maybe even 100. I was confused, overwhelmed, emotional, and distraught.

The next few months were a blur of visits, prayers, tears, and then finally, the call in the early morning hours on February 20, 2007 that she had peacefully passed away. I was shocked and speechless. *My grief landscape crumbled.*

A few short years later my father passed somewhat unexpectedly. One day he was at home on the phone, excitedly talking to me about his next trip with his newfound friend, Betty. The next day he was in the hospital, in a coma, facing death. I was able to rush to his bedside, pray with him, tell him how much I loved him, and be near him—I stayed up all night by his bedside.

The next day we brought him home from the hospital and he died early in the morning in his home on January 1, 2011. I felt lost, lonely, confused, and hurt—again, prayers, shock, pain, and a flood of tears.

For many years as an adult, I believed if my world fell apart around me, I could always go back to my parents' home and be OK. I would have a bed to sleep on and food to eat, and now that was no longer possible. A 50-year-old foundation was gone. My older brother Craig, said at the funeral, *"I feel like an orphan."*

Helen Keller said this about grief, "the only way to get to the other side is to go through the door." These events started a personal grief journey for me and led to the *Grief Journey* groups and this book. I decided to open wide the door.

WHAT SHOULD I EXPECT ON MY GRIEF JOURNEY?

In the 1970s Elizabeth Kübler-Ross' grief research[1] exploded on the grief scene with her "stages" theory. Her excellent work was actually directed toward those facing a terminal disease and their journey of dying—not particularly for the griever. This has led to some misunderstandings on the grief journey for many and made it more difficult to individualize the experience. Recent grief research has moved beyond the stage theory for grievers and incorporated a more holistic approach to this complex and difficult field.

While there seem to be no set stages in grief, there are often common responses we may deal with. We typically experience concentration issues, along with numbness, sleeping problems, eating and emotional issues, mental and physical concerns. Grief tends to come in waves, not stages. Normally, there are not time frames to predict or other absolutes that forecast your journey. The grief journey is an individual walk, best traveled among your God, fellow grievers, family, and friends.

I've found that the grief journey involves four dynamic areas:

1. **Resolution of emotional issues with our loved ones that may interfere with the normal grieving process.** Almost universally, grievers have unresolved issues, events or communications with their departed loved ones that cry out for resolution. Resolution often involves great pain and discomfort. This may include hurts from or toward your loved one. You will benefit greatly by traveling this grief journey for yourself, for your own sanity, and your emotional well-being and health. As you might guess, this will not be your last loss and this "first time around" will teach you many important lessons for future losses.

2. **There is an opportunity to draw close to God in ways that are not available outside of walking your grief journey.** You will have the opportunity to find a compassionate, concerned, and loving God in the grieving process and developing a new and different relationship with him which translates into energy and motivation to live lives dedicated to God and our loved ones. As you read this book, there is an opportunity to draw close to God in ways that are not available outside of walking your grief journey.

3. **Entering into an *enduring relationship* with your loved one.** Our world is never the same after losing a loved one. Many things change and it is vital that we adjust to this new reality. An enduring relationship is the final work done in the *Grief Journey* group. This biblical concept is also, a more comforting, energizing, and honoring way to view the loss of our loved ones. The grief journey is an opportunity to honor our loved one and the influence they've had in our life. *Often after a significant loss, we too quickly move on and thus dishonor the impact of a life well lived.*

4. **An ability to assist others with grief and loss issues.** William Penn once said, "For death is no more than a turning of us over from time to eternity"—not something we stop, get rid of, or ever get used to. Our society (and the church worldwide) often struggles with how to grieve well. We have the opportunity to be a "pioneer of compassion" and a help to many others in the coming years. Others need our experience and compassion as they face this life-changing event. By our engagement in *Grief Journey*, we will be equipped to be a caring friend to others.

Grief Journey addresses all four of these important areas.

The grief journey is different for everyone. There is an overall agreement among researchers[2] that the grief journey entails three essential elements:

- **Shock and Numbness**

- **Disorganization**

- **Restructuring**

Shock and Numbness: The first phase of grief, shock and numbness, is characterized by an outright denial of the death. Many survivors have little recall of the funeral or who was present following a death. Others remember everything remarkably, as if they were viewing it through an opaque lens.

Others still, refuse to believe that the death has taken place. Survivors may feel a sense of anxiety, sadness, and fatigue. This phenomenon is actually a healthy response of our body to protect us, which allows us time to take in this devastating event before we dive into the long and often arduous grief journey.

Disorganization: In the second phase of grief, disorganization, there is emotional disarray, along with physical and mental upheaval. The mourner may feel anxious, angry, fearful, depressed, and angst-ridden. Other common feelings include guilt, relief, agitation, or even reverting back to a denial stance, which may last for some time. Feelings may fluctuate during this time with periods of normality alternating with extreme sadness and even deep depression. This is all quite normal and not unexpected.

I often hear of the griever during and after this time, "Oh they're doing really well." The griever may appear strong, sharp, and even at peace. This is often concerning, as stuffing emotions and denying feelings may lead to years of struggle and difficulty in the grief journey. As difficult as engaging these emotions are, discussing your loss and, allowing yourself the freedom to do so, will make a difficult time, easier. "Leaning into the pain" is often the smartest, most effective, and quickest way through this journey.

Restructuring: In the third phase of grief, restructuring, we learn to develop new roles and responsibilities, relationships, and skills. Indeed, it is virtually impossible to not do so, as we've now entered into a new world—one without our loved one. We learn to readjust to our new reality, taking the time to appreciate the lasting memories of our loved one, with the goal to fully integrate and invest back into a "normal" life.

These three phases are intertwined, connected, and related to each other. Those of us on a grief journey may tend to travel back and forth between them for as long as we need to, walking this new journey–stumbling or lost at times, sometimes venturing off the trail, only to find ourselves back again. Eventually, a new life of hope emerges.

> "Grief seems to come in waves—and quite unexpected at times! Sometimes as a tsunami and other times in gentle, lapping waves—small reminders, tugs of nostalgic memories— often with tears and now, frequently with a smile."

THE OPPORTUNITY TO INTIMATELY KNOW GOD

Grief presents an open door for God to express himself to us in unique and unexpected ways. He uses our grief journey to demonstrate his love, reveal his character, heal our hearts, and remind us of the brevity of all life.

This book is written within the framework of the Scriptures, with Jesus, as our model of the suffering savior, the Holy Spirit as a guiding hand, and God the Father, who has a heart for the griever. He created you as an emotional being with the capacity to feel deeply, and you have the God-given right to express those thoughts and emotions to others to find healing. If Christians can't grieve like God grieves, then who can?

Grief humbles us. We are no longer in full control of our lives (as if we ever were) and there are things that we will never be able to influence again. On the day I was informed of my mother's terminal illness, I collapsed in tears on the stairway, as I was going upstairs, and pleaded for my mom's life—*"Please God, do something, do anything to make this awful story stop."* I have a need to control my world, to understand why things have to happen and why they cannot be prevented. Death takes that away—I don't understand and probably never will—death is complex and not easily explained, and if someone tries to do so, beware.

Grief seems to come in waves and not stages. One day, while sitting in the neighborhood rec center's locker room—totally unaware of any thoughts that day about my mom, I broke down and wept. Nothing happened that day to remind me of her. No special anniversary or event—just a regular day. Grief seems to come in waves—and quite unexpected at times. Sometimes as a tsunami and other times in gentle, lapping waves—small reminders, tugs of nostalgic memories—often with tears and now, frequently with a smile.

Many issues that arrive with grief and loss have little to do with a cognitive problem—that is, something is wrong with our thinking or some kind of mental health diagnosis. I've witnessed an increase of private counseling being suggested for those in the grips of unresolved grief. Rather, as Russell Friedman and John James state in the *Grief Recovery Handbook*, "grief is an issue of a broken heart not a broken mind." And where better to deal with our broken hearts than the local church?

Yes, there is a cognitive journey to be traveled in our grief. Learning some of the features of grief—myths, commonalities, and God's perspective is essential. But much of the grief journey is a journey of the heart—*the healing of a broken and shattered heart.* The grief journey will take great patience, grace that allows for mistakes, courage to keep going, family, and friends to carry you at times and, faith and trust in a compassionate, caring, and loving God.

Solomon reminds us to, above all else guard your heart (Proverbs 4:23)—grief has a way of defining the direction of a heart. Some in their grief find themselves diminished in living a full life—as if something died inside of us. We might become jaded. We may think, *"If we all just die someday, then what's the use in investing in life?"* While we usually won't verbalize this, we may live this way. We lose our zest for life. Dreams may wither away or areas that were once significant lose their importance. Or at best, we simply ignore our loss with a nonchalant shrug of our shoulders—a metaphor for life. On the other hand, some choose to engage grief and in the process become emotionally fuller and equipped to help other grievers.

> **"Grief presents an open door for God to express himself to us in unexpected ways. He uses our grief to demonstrate his love, reveal his character, heal our hearts and remind us of the brevity of all life."**

TIME AND SPACE

I'm a huge ice hockey fan. Often the announcer makes this comment about the defenseman bringing the puck up the ice to create a play: *"Bringing the puck up the ice, he has time and space to make the play"*—two important concepts to create a good play in hockey—time and space. Grief recovery is like that. In order to properly grieve we need both time and space.

Many of us do not take the time or develop space to grieve and mourn. We learn of the news of a death, we attend the funeral or memorial service, spend time with family, and then often quickly go back to our normal routines and never find the time or the space to properly grieve. All of us need the time and a safe and confidential space to open up, share our hearts, be listened to, and offer assistance to others.

TIME TO GRIEVE

"Your group gave me the luxury to grieve," Lisa mentioned as we left group one day. I was not sure at first what she meant. *The luxury to grieve?"* Then she explained: "After my father died, I attended the funeral and then came back home to my kids and job—life just kept going and I never took the time to grieve. Your group offered me the luxury to grieve. I took 90 minutes a week to focus on what was important to me and it helped tremendously."

We must take the time to consider the lost relationship, face the pain of grief, and work through perhaps the most challenging journey of our life. Grief is a time and energy-consuming event. *There is no substitute for taking the needed time to grieve.*

We make excuses. We forget. (I once did that with a tooth problem and it resulted in an abscessed tooth and a costly and painful root canal) We fill up our lives so we don't have to feel. Who wants to "re-feel" the pain of a loss by attending a group? The problem with this thinking is that if we don't go through the grief journey we feel the pain in many other ways: disconnected relationships, unresolved issues with a "low fever" kind of pain, by not properly grieving. This may show up in many areas of life–our walk with God, our friendships, in our marriage, and family dynamics. Just like my tooth issue— it's pay me now or pay me later!

We may give in to old habits or addictions to numb the pain and make us feel better for a time, instead of taking the time to grieve. Please, take time to grieve, as God would have you grieve. Time that will not only help you and others but also honor the one you've lost.

SPACE TO GRIEVE

We find the space to grieve by spending time in a group of nonjudgmental friends and a confidential place to share some of our deepest emotional baggage. To be with like-minded sojourners who can walk with us, speak our language of grief, and lead us through a sometimes-bewildering place is essential for us to travel this journey.

Grief visits us—often in tragic, sudden and unexpected ways. It is an unfortunate and difficult part of the human experience, something every human must work through.

But grieving in a public space can be uncomfortable and a bit unsettling. Having a safe and confidential place is essential. Knowing that a group "has your back" to allow you to feel what you feel or to say whatever you need to say, without judgment or insensitivity, is paramount as we walk this grief journey. Hopefully, you will find such a group. Appendix E explains how one may lead a *Grief Journey* group.

HOW TO USE THIS BOOK

What losses do grievers bring to this book? Certainly, those of our loved ones—spouses, children, parents, siblings, coworkers, and friends. Many find solace with the Grief Journey while mourning the loss of unborn children, marriages, and other relationships. Finally, some will find this book useful in dealing with the loss of a pet, careers, dreams, and related losses. You may need to adjust some of the concepts in the book to fit these special kinds of losses.

The sojourner metaphor is a common one and one that I find fits well with the grief journey. A sojourner is one who travels. The Free Dictionary[3] describes sojourner as: "temporary stay," "visit," "stay," or "dwell for a time." The grief journey is one where we visit, stay for a while, and then move on. It is not as if we live in grief the rest of our lives, however we are never the same. But to move on, we must travel with grief, stay for some time, understand and experience the environment and then, when ready, we continue our travels.

JOURNALING

What we work out in our journals we don't take out on our family and friends. —C.S. Lewis

An essential part of the grief journey is personal journaling. At the end of each chapter you will find a **Digging Deeper** section to journal in. Please take time each week to work on these questions as they will help you in your journey and also compose much of the discussion in the group setting. Here are a few reasons to journal

- The grief journey is difficult to process simply in our heads–journaling allows us to get grief "out in front" of us, to more effectively deal with our questions, emotions, and hurts.

- Journaling helps us to develop a record of vital thoughts to return to at later dates.

- Journaling provides a template for conversation during recovery with our friends.

- Journaling is an effective and compassionate way to honor our loved one.

- Consider the book, *Five Years: When Someone We Loved Had Cancer,* by Ally Publico (CARE Foundation) as a resource on effective journaling.

Finally, this book is best used in conjunction with a *Grief Journey* group. A compassionate Christian and fellow sojourner will lead groups. *Grief Journey* groups meet for 90 minutes weekly and last eight weeks.

If, however, you are not able to attend a group or are not ready to do so, *Grief Journey* may be used as a helpful guide to walk the grief journey by yourself.

Here are a few suggestions for those who do not attend a group:

- Prayerfully consider your ability to walk this journey on your own.

- Carve out ample time (at least an hour) each week to read and journal.

- Find a safe and confidential friend (preferably one who has traveled the grief journey before) to share your journal with. Ask this friend for a weekly commitment to listen to you and offer support.

A few closing thoughts before you begin this journey: During this time, you may have some unique needs that you must take care of. Grief recovery is often a difficult journey that can be spiritually, socially, physically, and emotionally taxing. Perhaps, let your trusted friends know you are doing this. Some feel like they are being selfish by traveling down this road—that there are more important things to do. Jesus didn't think so—he modeled for us how a "Suffering Savior" lives. *Be good to yourself.*

Consider not making any big life changes (diet, starting a new educational journey, etc.) as the grief journey will require much energy. Get plenty of sleep, eat well, and exercise—these are vital to any kind of recovery and especially the grief journey you are embarking on. *Take care of yourself.*

Try not to judge yourself harshly and *never compare and minimalize*[4] your experience or feelings. I've thought things like, "Well I did have my mother for 50 years and that's better than someone else who may have lost their mother earlier to a tragedy." When and how I lost my mom is not the issue. All of our experiences are vastly different from anyone else's because we have a wide array of experiences with our loved one, so don't compare your journey to others. *Be kind to yourself.*

Note: Some may have complicated grief issues (when grief is combined with a mental health diagnosis) and need more support and intervention than a group or this book provides. Complicated grief may be present if you have many unresolved losses in your life, have an inability to express strong emotions, or there is a history of mental health issues that are not improving.

Attend your church group, but also stay open to the need for further help. I suggest private counseling or involvement in a longer-term grief group in addition to attending a *Grief Journey* group. The "Resources" page in the back of the book, may prove helpful.

END NOTES

[1] Dr. Elisabeth Kubler-Ross wrote her seminal work, *On Death and Dying*, to offer us a new perspective on the terminally ill. It is not a psychoanalytic study, nor is it a "how-to" manual for grieving. Rather, it refocuses on the terminally ill patient as a human being and a teacher, in the hope that we will learn from them about the final stages of life.

[2] William Worden is a grief counselor and wrote a seminal work for therapists: *Grief Counseling and Grief Therapy, Fourth Edition: A Handbook for the Mental Health Practitioner 4th Edition*, Springer Publishing, 2009. Other prominent researchers are Colin Murray Parkes, psychologist John Bowlby, Dr. Roberta Temes and Geoffrey Gorer, among others.

[3] http://www.thefreedictionary.com/sojourner

[4] *Grief and Trauma in Children: An Evidence-Based Treatment Manual*, Alison Salloum.

Digging Deeper

Questions I have about grief: _____

_____

_____

_____

Fears I have as I begin this journey: _____

_____

_____

_____

What will grief recovery look like for me? _____

_____

_____

Who do I know that I can talk to about my grief? _____

_____

The *Grief Journey* Group:

   Day/Time: _____

   Location: _____

What I may need to do to prepare for this journey: _____

_____

_____

*Yet the Lord longs to be gracious to you; therefore he will rise up
to show you compassion. For the Lord is a God of justice.
Blessed are all who wait for him!* —Isaiah 30:18

JOURNALING _____

_____

_____

_____

_____

_____

_____

_____

_____

_____

_____

_____

_____

_____

_____

_____

_____

_____

_____

_____

_____

_____

_____

_____

_____

_____

_____

_____

_____

_____

JOURNALING

_____

_____

_____

_____

_____

_____

_____

_____

_____

_____

_____

_____

_____

_____

_____

_____

_____

_____

_____

_____

_____

_____

_____

CHAPTER ONE

JESUS EMBRACES GRIEF—WILL YOU?

Jesus wept. —John 11:35

I knew this was going to be difficult. I flew immediately from Denver to my parents' home on the East Coast after my mom passed away to be with family for the memorial service. I was still in a state of shock, and disoriented, and did not know what to expect. The whole family was there—brothers and sister, and their spouses, children, and friends—I was quite overwhelmed and tempted to shut down emotionally. Fortunately, I refused this temptation and walked into a wall of emotional drama that would forever change my life. I decided to fully embrace my grief journey.

Upon entering the front door, I was shocked to hear my mother's voice coming out of the kitchen, among others. It was a voice as clear and as familiar as it had ever been. How could this be? My mind knew she was gone but my emotions and ears were hearing otherwise—was I going crazy?

Often, when we lose a loved one, our world becomes wonky, unstable, and unpredictable, and we may even doubt our senses and ourselves. Time may seem to stand still or fly by. Perhaps we lose energy and a will to go on. Our concentration may become limited and we lose sleep or sleep too much. Some experience conflicting feelings such as guilt, relief, anger, confusion, and resentment at your loved one's negative influences, while sad that they are now gone.

We may become depressed or sad and the sadness does not lift. Other emotions such as rage, isolation, confusion, anxiety, disappointment, jealousy, incompetence, vindictiveness, fear, envy, anguish, dismay, betrayal, rejection and apathy, may take root. Jesus, who experienced every challenge we face, can identify with our emotions.

Some have suicidal thoughts or emotional outbursts when not expected. Our moods may change without warning. Maybe we revert to drinking alcohol or drugs to deaden the pain or return to a previous addiction to find relief.

Others simply feel powerless in their daily lives and cannot seem to gain any sense of reasonable control. Questions like, "Will I feel like this forever?" take up residence in our confused state.

I sometimes found myself crying at random times and around people I didn't know very well. Experiencing and demonstrating strong emotions is not a sign of weakness but of strength and love. *Emotional displays are a sign of being fully human.* Grief, crying, and emotions[1] are the cost we pay for loving someone. We know our pain and fortunately, Jesus understands, cares about, and empathizes with our pain.

Learning to "Hold the Moment"

Mother's Day is always difficult for me when attending church. Mothers get honored with flowers and an emotional "Mama" song, and I usually feel quite sad and alone. The first few Mother's Day occasions after my mom's passing, I simply walked out to the foyer for that part of the service and then returned later. This year I made a decision to "hold the moment" that is, to stay with my emotions and simply allow them to be. I had learned this concept in my counseling of others. When my clients become very emotional, I am tempted to try and "fix" them by saying something soothing or positive, instead of simply allowing them to experience the emotions they have. I decided to apply this to myself. It was a challenge to hold this moment but I realized it would be fine and the emotions would eventually pass and I could move on. Try it. When you feel really tempted to "fix" an emotional event (whether yours or a friend's), simply stay quiet and allow the moment to occur—just let it be. Hold the moment.

JESUS ENGAGES GRIEF

He was despised and rejected by mankind, a man of suffering, and familiar with pain. Like one from whom people hide their face, he was despised, and we held him in low esteem. —Isaiah 53:3

Jesus was a man well aware of grief. As the Son of God and Son of Man, he had plenty to keep him busy—sin to confront, hearts to change, truth to reveal, healings to perform, disciples to train, and a gruesome death to die. And yet Jesus periodically took the time to grieve—to engage a process of pain, hurt, and healing. We should too.

What is the proper way to react to devastation? Is there a "proper"? Let's look at the perfect man and how he handled grief issues. Jesus—a man acquainted with grief illustrates what living life fully engaged looks like. Let's look at a snapshot of this "Man of Sorrows."

On his arrival, Jesus found that Lazarus had already been in the tomb for four days. Now Bethany was less than two miles from Jerusalem, and many Jews had come to Martha and Mary to comfort them in the loss of their brother. When Martha heard that Jesus was coming, she went out to meet him, but Mary stayed at home.

"Lord," Martha said to Jesus, "if you had been here, my brother would not have died. But I know that even now God will give you whatever you ask."

Jesus said to her, "Your brother will rise again."

Martha answered, "I know he will rise again in the resurrection at the last day."

Jesus said to her, "I am the resurrection and the life. The one who believes in me will live, even though they die; and whoever lives by believing in me will never die. Do you believe this?"

"Yes, Lord," she replied, "I believe that you are the Messiah, the Son of God, who is to come into the world."

After she had said this, she went back and called her sister Mary aside. "The Teacher is here," she said, "and is asking for you." When Mary heard this, she got up quickly and went to him. Now Jesus had not yet entered the village, but was still at the place where Martha had met him. When the Jews who had been with Mary in the house, comforting her, noticed how quickly she got up and went out, they followed her, supposing she was going to the tomb to mourn there.

When Mary reached the place where Jesus was and saw him, she fell at his feet and said, "Lord, if you had been here, my brother would not have died.

When Jesus saw her weeping, and the Jews who had come along with her also weeping, he was deeply moved in spirit and troubled. "Where have you laid him?" he asked.

"Come and see, Lord," they replied.

Jesus wept.

Then the Jews said, "See how he loved him!

"But some of them said, "Could not he who opened the eyes of the blind man have kept this man from dying?"

Jesus, once more deeply moved, came to the tomb. It was a cave with a stone laid across the entrance. "Take away the stone," he said.

"But, Lord," said Martha, the sister of the dead man, "by this time there is a bad odor, for he has been there four days."

Then Jesus said, "Did I not tell you that if you believe, you will see the glory of God?"

So they took away the stone. Then Jesus looked up and said, "Father, I thank you that you have heard me. I knew that you always hear me, but I said this for the benefit of the people standing here, that they may believe that you sent me."

When he had said this, Jesus called in a loud voice, "Lazarus, come out!" The dead man came out, his hands and feet wrapped with strips of linen, and a cloth around his face.

Jesus said to them, "Take off the grave clothes and let him go." —John 11:17-44

Allow me to clear a myth up right away. A common response I hear about Jesus in this story is: Of course, Jesus knew he would raise Lazarus from the dead, so this was not a big deal to him. That is, Jesus, being fully God, knew he would raise Lazarus from the dead, so this was just some kind of show. It didn't really hurt much for him since he knew in advance he would see Lazarus again, alive. "Well, hold on a minute."

So, were his tears somehow fake? Did he not feel his grief? Was his weeping staged? Are we saying Jesus was not authentic in this situation? The answer is an emphatic no! Jesus wept—the shortest verse in the Bible, but packed with compassion, emotion, and drama—he did feel his grief deeply over the loss of his friend and he was not afraid to completely express his grief—Jesus fully engaged his grief.

I am reminded of the time I had to put my basset hound Brewski to sleep after his valiant fight with cancer. While I've scoffed at the kinds of money, emotion, and time some spend on their pets, when it's *your pet*—all bets are off. Losing my pal Brewski was hard. The same goes for Jesus and Lazarus. Lazarus was just a character in the Bible to all of us, but to Jesus—he was a close and intimate friend (see John 12:1). This loss hurt and Jesus, no stranger to sorrow, fully engages his grief.

As always, Jesus models the perfect way to handle grief—authentic and vulnerable. Be inspired in your grief journey by Jesus' example.

> **"When we refuse to fully engage our grief, we become strangers to others' grief."**

Jesus embraced grief. There is a difference between being dragged along in our grief, kicking and screaming, and actively engaging it. Some reluctantly go along for the ride—they are often taken over by their grief and grief takes them where it will.

Whether we know it or not, the grief journey changes us. Some, who rarely pay attention to their losses, unwittingly say things like, "Oh, I'm over it now" or "It wasn't a big deal." Others, knowing they need to attend to their grief and are fearful of the unknown, simply put it off for another time. That "another time" rarely comes.

Jesus instead, engaged his grief. He waded right into it and found himself fully engrossed in the drama of Lazarus' passing. Right off the bat, you sense that Jesus was authentically feeling every emotion. Because he fully engaged his own grief, he became aware of the pain others felt. I've become a much better grief counselor, having engaged the pain of my parents' passing. When we refuse to fully engage our grief, we become strangers to others' grief.

Engagement takes a decision. We have to resolve to lean into our grief, count the cost of the challenges that lie ahead, and make time and space in our heart to engage grief. Jesus had many things to do, people to see and the world to win, but he took the time, created the space, and expended the energy needed to engage his grief.

Jesus fully felt the loss of his loved one. Never one to go along with society's desire to withhold his emotions, Jesus allowed himself to fully experience the pain of losing his friend, Lazarus and the drama of Mary and Martha's grief. He unashamedly felt the painful emotions of his friend's death.

Jesus was fully present during this emotional time and did not care about how he might appear to others. Would his "weakness" of expressing his pain cause them to struggle in their relationship with God? No, just the opposite—Jesus' grief draws us to him. Of Jesus, the scripture is true—*For when I am weak, then I am strong.* (2 Corinthians 12:10) Take this time to learn to be in touch with your feelings of grief. Imitate Jesus, decide to engage and embrace grief.

Jesus understood how we "bargain with God" over the loss of a loved one. While our society tells us to "hurry up and get over it," Jesus spent time allowing Mary and Martha to question God's plan for them, his ways, and his sovereignty. Death comes in many forms, at a variety of times and is often shocking to our view of a loving and caring God. Death can cause us to question God, his motives, his plans and his timing.

Questioning God and his ways during times of grief is normal and expected. Jesus did not correct or admonish the sisters. He stayed with them, engaged in the drama of the moment, and then offered help. In times of loss we have the choice to either draw close to God in trust and obedience, or pull away from him in anger, hurt, and confusion. Grief often brings God into a sharper focus despite the stresses of life.

Jesus embodied what it was like to live in a fallen world and the range of human emotions. Jesus understands when we suffer loss and how such loss redefines us and, if we let it, eventually makes us "whole" again. We become new people with new experiences. Life will never be the same once we experience loss, but our life doesn't have to be colored negatively because of our loss. This is a choice we make, and much of that depends on how we choose to grieve. We can either engage and direct our grief and mourning or have it direct us—either way we are going in a new direction. There are many good books on engaging loss— consider Mitch Albom's inspiring works[2].

Jesus leaned into the pain of his loss. He did not wander around the peripheries of the situation, closely measuring his responses and emotions. No, Jesus leaned into his pain. Jesus didn't treat his grief like some kind of mental disease but as a deeply troubling experience that he needed God the Father to help him work through.

We have the opportunity to lean into our grief. Yes, this is difficult and the emotional journey is fraught with uncertainty. But it is the only way to a healed heart. Engaging our grief is not weakness, but strength. If we can't cry over losing a loved one, then when can we cry? Refuse to buy into the destructive lie that "Real men don't cry." Jesus cried, even wept, so let's be like Jesus. Followers of Jesus—people of faith—should fully experience loss.

Typical grievers are not strange, have some kind of deficient cognitive issue, or out of the norm—we are the norm. Loss is an event we all must face. Grief is a normal life experience; it is the journey of the broken hearted that demands the attentiveness by the individual griever and the care, empathy, wisdom, love, and compassion imparted from fellow travelers who have blazed the trail before.

> "Jesus was a man well aware of grief. As the Son of God and Son of Man, he had plenty to keep him busy—sin to confront, hearts to change, truth to reveal, healings to perform, disciples to train and a gruesome death to die. And yet Jesus periodically took time to grieve— to engage a process of pain, hurt and healing. We should too."

Jesus served in his grief. While he was hurt over the loss of Lazarus, Jesus also realized others were hurting as well and he drew upon his relationship with God to serve them. He tended to the sisters' hurts and questions. He patiently shared his own hurt and even taught a bit of a lesson on the afterlife.

I was so moved by my sister Sandy and brother Curtis as they moved into my parents' home for several weeks as my mom was in home hospice. They spent countless hours serving her and the rest of us. They cared and loved before I knew what to do. Once I was able to join in, I found great comfort in serving as well. When we don't know what else to do, serve.

Jesus took his grief to the social realm. Jesus demonstrates the difference between grieving and mourning. Grieving is dealing with the pain of a loss within you. Your feelings, emotions, pain, and mental challenges that come with an upheaval like death. Mourning is living the loss among others—it is grief socially expressed. Jesus felt no need to "protect" those in grief by withholding his. He was able to fully experience his grief among his best friends—this is how we best honor our loved ones and travel the long and often difficult grief journey.

Jesus openly expressed his own extreme emotions and sorrow (John 11:33, 35). He embraced (different from "allowing" grief to happen) his broken heart—he found comfort, strength, and purpose in his grief with friends, family and God.

CONCLUSION

Jesus amazes me every time I read about and contemplate him. He perfects every facet of life. Even in his sorrow, Jesus demonstrates how we "do" grief. Jesus embraced and embodied grief with honesty, emotion, vulnerability, and compassion for others by fully engaging his loss and leaning into his pain—he even served in his grief. He was vulnerable and honest—Jesus took an extremely difficult private event, an awkward social situation, and showed the world how to respond like God would. In our personal grief journey, we can strive to follow the example Jesus set for us in the area of personal grieving and in his empathy for others.

END NOTES

[1] If you struggle with vulnerability watch this Ted Talk by Brene' Brown: http://www.ted.com/talks/brene_brown_on_vulnerability.

[2] Mitch Albom is a former sports writer for the Detroit Free Press, who turned his life around by writing. He is a best-selling author, journalist, screenwriter, playwright, radio and television broadcaster, and musician. I found *Tuesdays With Morrie: An Old, A Young Man and Life's Greatest Lessons* and *For One More Day* to be particularly helpful in my engagement of grief. His books have sold over 35 million copies.

Digging Deeper

What prompted you to buy this book or join the *Grief Journey* group?

_____

_____

_____

What would you like to learn or grow in during the next several
weeks? _____

_____

_____

_____

What have you done so far to engage your grief? _____

_____

_____

_____

How can you best prepare for this grief journey? _____

_____

_____

_____

_____

_____

"Do not let your hearts be troubled. You believe in God; believe also in me.
—John 14:1

JOURNALING _____

_____

_____

_____

_____

_____

_____

_____

_____

_____

_____

_____

_____

_____

_____

_____

_____

_____

_____

_____

_____

_____

_____

_____

_____

_____

_____

_____

JOURNALING

JOURNALING _____

_____

_____

_____

_____

_____

_____

_____

_____

_____

_____

_____

_____

_____

_____

_____

_____

_____

_____

_____

_____

_____

_____

_____

CHAPTER TWO

THE FATHER'S HEART FOR THE GRIEVER

Meanwhile, where is God? This is one of the most disquieting symptoms. When you are happy, so happy that you have no sense of needing him, so happy that you are tempted to feel his claims upon you are an interruption, if you re-member yourself and turn to him with gratitude and praise, you will be—or so it feels—welcomed with open arms. But go to him when your need is desperate, when all other help is vain, and what do you find? A door slammed in your face, and a sound of bolting and double bolting on the inside. After that, silence. You may as well turn away. The longer you wait, the more empathic the silence will become. There are no lights in the windows. – C.S. Lewis in *A Grief Observed*[1]

I received a phone call one afternoon that my mom's cancer was terminal and she had only a short time left to live. I felt powerless, abandoned, and forsaken. I prayed, but did so with a disorganized mind, confused heart, and unsteady legs. That night I stayed home by myself, hurting, crying, and con-fused. At one point as I walked upstairs, I fell to my knees in the stairway and pleaded with God for her life. Even in my tears, I knew this grief wasn't going away anytime soon. I was humbled. The psalmist captured my heart:

I went about mourning as though for my friend or brother. I bowed my head in grief as though weeping for my mother. —Psalm 35:14

Have you ever felt this way? Grief visits you unexpectedly and during your most difficult time, God is seemingly nowhere to be found? You pray or cry out and hear a deafening silence.

The grief journey may represent an important juncture in our walk with God. It represents a time to either distance ourselves from God or draw close to him. We may cynically question God, perhaps pull our hearts back and, foster distrust for him. Some have lost or seriously damaged their faith because of unresolved grief. By contrast, our grief journey may become a time to intimately draw near to God in ways we never expected, explored, or experienced.

Each heart knows its own bitterness and no one else can share its joy. —Proverbs 14:10

Friends and family often help us in our grief journey and are a vital part of our recovery. They have their role in our journey, but only God reaches into the depths of our soul and heart for true healing. Despite the inability of others to fully connect with you to heal in your grief—God can and does. God is the father of compassion and is yearning to reach out and heal his children. Healing the grief-stricken soul is the very heart of our God. Consider and contemplate the following verses:

But you, God, see the trouble of the afflicted; you consider their grief and take it in hand. The victims commit themselves to you; you are the helper of the fatherless.
—Psalm 10:14

Though he brings grief, he will show compassion, so great is his unfailing love.
—Lamentations 3:32

And he passed in front of Moses, proclaiming, "The Lord, the Lord, the compassionate and gracious God, slow to anger, abounding in love and faithfulness.
—Exodus 34:6

Your compassion, Lord, is great; preserve my life according to your laws.
—Psalm 119:156

Can a mother forget the baby at her breast and have no compassion on the child she has borne? Though she may forget, I will not forget you! —Isaiah 49:15

Because of the Lord's great love we are not consumed, for his compassions never fail. —Lamentations 3:22

Praise be to the God and Father of our Lord Jesus Christ, the Father of compassion and the God of all comfort, who comforts us in all our troubles, so that we can comfort those in any trouble with the comfort we ourselves receive from God. For just as we share abundantly in the sufferings of Christ, so also our comfort abounds through Christ. If we are distressed, it is for your comfort and salvation; if we are comforted, it is for your comfort, which produces in you patient endurance of the same sufferings we suffer. And our hope for you is firm, because we know that just as you share in our sufferings, so also you share in our comfort. —2 Corinthians 1:3-7

God has gone to great lengths to convince us of the comfort he provides in our grief. The words "care," "comfort," and "compassion" are found 400 times in the Bible. While you have family and friends to help you along this journey, take this opportunity to run to God for care, compassion, and comfort.

Remember, grief is a matter of a broken heart, not simply broken thinking. At times our friends and family may say things that are factually accurate yet emotionally desolate.[2] Their words are perhaps correct but they do little to calm and quiet the heart. Only God can fully soothe the soul. He speaks comfort into our troubled hearts. God and God alone comforts our hurting hearts and provides consolation, relief, and peace—only God can do this.

In this chapter, we will focus on God's heart for the griever, found in Psalm 31. Like the human Jesus, David was a man familiar with grief and suffering. David felt the pain of bitterness, loss, and loneliness that we all feel in grief. David could have embittered his heart, grown cynical, and wilted into the background, becoming a footnote in biblical history. But instead, David, a man after God's own heart, turned his attention to his loving Father and his heart for the griever.

Like David and Jesus, we have the ability, spirit, and prompting to turn to God in our greatest times of need. He knows grief, understands our hurts, and most important, is eagerly waiting to heal your heart.

1. God reveals himself in the middle of our pain.

In you, Lord, I have taken refuge; let me never be put to shame; deliver me in your righteousness. Turn your ear to me, come quickly to my rescue; be my rock of refuge, a strong fortress to save me. Since you are my rock and my fortress, for the sake of your name lead and guide me. Keep me free from the trap that is set for me, for you are my refuge. Into your hands I commit my spirit; deliver me, Lord, my faithful God. I hate those who cling to worthless idols; as for me, I trust in the Lord. I will be glad and rejoice in your love, for you saw my affliction and knew the anguish of my soul. You have not given me into the hands of the enemy but have set my feet in a spacious place. —Psalm 31:1-8

• **Run to God.** While grieving among our friends is essential for recovery, we want to prioritize who we run to and when. God should be who we first turn to, pray to, and look to for answers in crises. After we run to God, then we can turn to our friendships for help. Grief presents a unique opportunity to find God in a new way—perhaps one that we've never experienced before. David asked God to listen and come quickly to the rescue. God is acutely tuned in to our pleas for help during our grief journey.

We see this demonstrated over and over in the Bible. When facing dire challenges of the heart, God's people turn to him first, including Moses, Hannah, David, and Paul and are stellar examples of running to God, even Jesus turned toward heaven during his toughest times.

But in their distress they turned to the LORD, the God of Israel, and sought him, and he was found by them. —2 Chronicles 15:4

"Friends have their role but only God reaches into the depths of our soul and heart for healing. Despite the inability of others to fully connect with you to heal in your grief—God can and does."

Those of us who are parents know this to be true with our children. When our children are doing well, we're content as parents and life is fine. But when pain comes their way—a bruised knee, first romantic break up, or someone hurts them—we spring into action, our hearts engage like a lit match, and we run to the rescue. God is like that—when his children hurt, he draws close to us in unique and special ways.

> *I lift up my eyes to the hills—where does my help come from? My help comes from the LORD, the Maker of heaven and earth. He will not let your foot slip—he who watches over you will not slumber; indeed, he who watches over Israel will neither slumber nor sleep.* —Psalm 121:1-3

- **God is a fortress against the shame that we might experience.** Grief can create distance and shame among the best of friends, in a marriage, or in the family. Shame often creeps into our souls during grief. Sometimes shame may be attached to childhood issues as we navigate our loss and what this loss might mean for our future. Other times shame is attached to how we see ourselves—our esteem, confidence, and hope for a different future. Shame that is attached to our identity in a negative way is opposed to and opposite to the way the Bible define us.

Death often causes isolation and confusion about our connection and role with others. It may bring about painful memories that we had packed away and forgotten about. Drawing close to God as he draws close to us is a fortress—a high wall—against the shame we may experience.

- **God guides us for the sake of his name.** God is jealous for his name (Exodus 34:14) and he will always protect his name. He puts his own reputation on the line during our worst moments. What God promises, he delivers. Perhaps not in the manner we might expect or in the timeframe we desire, but he delivers. God claims to run to our rescue and we take him up on this promise. He rescued David in his distress, Daniel in his time of need, Job in his many losses, Peter in prison, and Jesus in his suffering—he'll rescue you as well.

For many of us the greatest need here is to view the Bible through new eyes. Perhaps promises of God that we just skated over in the past, now take on new meaning and potential. God is lifted up in our pain and he protects us in our hurt. God seeks glory for himself, even in our distress. Call on God to keep his promises in our pain and show himself compassionate. Consider these promises found in the Scriptures: Psalm 10:14, 88:1-2, Lamentations 3:32, John 16:20, and 1 Peter 1:6.

- **God will put us in a spacious place.** Some days are worse than others. Some days feel like the day we first heard the news of our loved one's passing. We're feeling the rawness all over again and we fear life will always be like this. God enters this time and assures us that we don't stay in this level of grief forever. Things get better. God brings relief. Friends help and we begin to emerge out of the shadows to a brighter future. God is faithful.

> **"What we don't know is greater than what we do know." God is big enough to live right in the middle of my pain" —Craig Lounsbrough[3]**

2. God is aware that we may feel numb, stuck or trapped in our emotions.

> *Be merciful to me, Lord, for I am in distress; my eyes grow weak with sorrow, my soul and body with grief. My life is consumed by anguish and my years by groaning; my strength fails because of my affliction, and my bones grow weak. Because of all my enemies, I am the utter contempt of my neighbors and an object of dread to my closest friends—those who see me on the street flee from me. I am forgotten as though I were dead; I have become like broken pottery. For I hear many whispering, "Terror on every side!" They conspire against me and plot to take my life. But I trust in you, Lord; I say, "You are my God." My times are in your hands; deliver me from the hands of my enemies, from those who pursue me.* —Psalm 31:9-15

Intense emotions are expected, common, and don't offend God. Remember, feelings are generally value neutral—they are neither good nor bad—they just are. It's what we do with our emotions that may carry moral value. Sadness and depression are common during times of grief.

Embrace your emotions during this time. Freely allow your emotions to come and be what they will be. God is not shocked or put off by them. He created you an emotional being and honors those who authentically display their feelings.

Feelings of shock and disbelief are to be expected. God may feel very distant. Again, Jesus models this phenomenon as he cried out on the cross—*My God, My God, why have you forsaken me?* (Matthew 27:46). This can be a difficult dance at times. While we want to fully engage and experience our emotions, we can't be carried by them and behave in an ungodly manner. Lashing out at others, isolating, returning to addictive behavior, or other negative responses only serve to complicate our journey and hurt those we love the most. Feeling distant from God may be our reality, but it's not God's. He is an *"ever present help in times of trouble"* (Psalm 46:1).

There is a difference between clinical depression and circumstantial sadness. If you feel your sadness has lingered too long, is severely disrupting your life or is unusually intense, please consult a physician or seek professional counseling help. Otherwise, you are like the rest of humanity and in the throes of grief and mourning. You are where you should be.

• **Grief may result in intense social issues.** Friends may not know what to say or just avoid us altogether. We may feel shame because of the isolation caused by friends who distance themselves. People are not sure what to say and instead of drawing close to the griever, they may distance themselves. Phone calls go unreturned, promises forgotten, and awkwardness creeps into relationships. In our pain we may stay home, draw inward, and detach.

We sometimes experience shame that leads to loneliness and isolation. God understands and intervenes. The God of Compassion comforts. He acknowledges our situation by shining his face on us. We cry out; God answers. We isolate; God answers our grief by sending us a loving friend or two.

• **Death and grief expose us to our own humanity.** Death is the final frontier of the topic of the meaning of life. Nothing brings to the forefront our own mortality than the death of a loved one. We may begin to question God in ways we never have before. We may say or do things that are uncharacteristic of our walk with God.

Grief may be a search for meaning or a recommitment to that search. You may lash out at others or God in anger—how could you allow this to happen? Remember the difference in feeling and honoring an emotion and acting out on that emotion. Jesus felt his emotions deeply but always acted in a righteous manner. Stay Calm and Seek God.

• **Death humbles us.** I am not in control. I remember the utter helplessness I felt on the day my brother Danny called me with the news that mom's cancer was terminal—there was nothing we could do. The best medical care didn't make a difference. Her lifetime of healthy living didn't matter.

Prayer didn't seem to make a difference. I was humbled.

The Western world prides itself on the ability to "make things happen." We live largely independent lives, rack up accolades for our achievements, and enjoy the best medical care the world has to offer. We feel invincible—and then death visits. All of our security vanishes and we are humbled.

Dealing with death has a way of reminding us we are not fully in charge of this life. We are given 60, 70, maybe 80 or so years to live our lives and then we're done. One preacher reminded me of this as he spoke of his parents' passing saying, "Now it's my turn to step up to the plate."

Our days may come to seventy years, or eighty, if our strength endures; yet the best of them are but trouble and sorrow, for they quickly pass, and we fly away.
—Psalm 90:10

This "humbling" is not always a bad or negative feature of our lives. Humility is a way to refocus our lives. It allows us to look to the Creator of life (Ecclesiastes 12) and consider his ways. Don't waste this opportunity. Reflect on your walk with God. Search the Scriptures for the answers you need to navigate not only your journey of grief but also your life going forward. Death often opens our hearts to new insights and motivations for living.

• Death can bring up deficits regarding unresolved childhood issues. Grieving is an emotionally draining process and we are often quite vulnerable during this time. We may revert back to our childhood roles—insecure, needy or take charge. Perhaps issues that we thought had been resolved years ago resurface and complicate matters. God knows and understands and has a heart for his people.

Engaging in the grief journey can reveal major issues on how we view God and thus an opportunity to see him as never before. Family dynamics are revealed and may need to be attended to. Take caution before entering into childhood dynamics right after a loss, which may best be dealt with when there is ample time and space to do so.

• We may have experienced a numbness or denial at the news. A common emotion that most of us experienced at the news of our loss was numbness. Some even say things like, "No way!" or" Really?" at the initial news. It's as if the reality of the situation is too much for us to bear and our minds protect us by denying the fact.

Even when we are expecting the news, we are often shocked. When my dad called me with the news of my mom's passing at 6 a.m. on February 20, my first words were, "Are you sure?" Even though I was expecting this call for weeks, it came as a shock and I was not ready for it. The next few days and weeks were a daze as I navigated the memorial service and then the difficult weeks afterward. It was as if life had been stripped away and I felt raw, exposed, and vulnerable.

> "It seems that numbness is God's way of clearing the heart and mind, sweeping aside all that would impede Him having a uniquely powerful encounter with us in an uniquely devastating time. It makes for an empty room cleared of everything except two chairs and time. Numbness is God's invitation to intimacy in crisis." —Craig Lounsbrough

3. Grief has the potential to create intimacy or distance with God.

> *Let your face shine on your servant; save me in your unfailing love. Let me not be put to shame, Lord, for I have cried out to you; but let the wicked be put to shame and be silent in the realm of the dead. Let their lying lips be silenced, for with pride and contempt they speak arrogantly against the righteous. How abundant are the good things that you have stored up for those who fear you, that you bestow in the sight of all, on those who take refuge in you. In the shelter of your presence you hide them from all human intrigues; you keep them safe in your dwelling from accusing tongues. Praise be to the Lord, for he showed me the wonders of his love when I was in a city under siege. In my alarm I said, "I am cut off from your sight!" Yet you heard my cry for mercy when I called to you for help. Love the Lord, all his faithful people! The Lord preserves those who are true to him, but the proud he pays back in full. Be strong and take heart, all you who hope in the Lord.* —Psalm 31:16-24

• Grief at times may produce unexpected emotions or shame.

Perhaps we feel like we did something wrong or actually caused a death. During times of prolonged illness of our loved one, we may wish for this nightmare to be over and then, after our loved one dies, we are ashamed of our thoughts. Guilt and regret—blaming yourself for words that you never got to say, or actions you never were able to do, or dealing with things you did say and do. Sometimes we experience relief that they are no longer struggling and "messing up our life." Perhaps we experience seemingly inappropriate emotions such as apathy, laughing, relief, or ambivalence. Try to accept that these emotions and thoughts are part of a confusing and difficult time in your life and nothing more.

- **Our grief brings us into an intimacy with God.** Life presents us with an opportunity to draw close to God in new and unique ways—grief becomes an intimate call from God. His words in the Scriptures like *cleft of a rock, palm of his hand, safety…a refuge* take on new meaning. God not only protects us from shame but also brings us close to him during times of grief and mourning. We feel vulnerable and raw and at times others cannot meet such deep and probing needs, but God can. We find a *peace that transcends understanding,* (Philippians 4:7) that only God gives. The grief journey is often an opportunity to open us to the grace and mercy of God in new, creative, and faithful ways.

- **We must grasp the limits of our understanding.** Often we feel the need to "explain" God and his workings. How does one explain death? One of the reasons he even shows his wonders is so we cannot explain him. If we could explain everything about God, then he ceases to be God—he becomes just another one of man's creations.

Death is a phenomenon of God that escapes our full explanation (Proverbs 25:2). It may be that God wants it so. Beware of him who has all the answers to death—distance yourself from those who "know" all of God's thoughts about this mystery. Perhaps God is more interested in us living among the living and not the dead (Luke 24:5).

> *God's voice thunders in marvelous ways; he does great things beyond our understanding.* —Job 37:5
>
> *My heart is not proud, Lord, my eyes are not haughty; I do not concern myself with great matters or things too wonderful for me.* —Psalm 131:1

- **A call to action that produces hope.** God hears our personal cry for help in times of grief. He is waiting for us to call him forth into our grief journey. There is an engagement that takes place as we begin to seek after the very Creator of Life.

Our tendency may be to "just move on" and get back to life. Many of us refuse to engage grief after a loss. We strive to have things as normal—the way things were before. We distract ourselves, keep busy and act as if nothing happened. But God beckons us into action with our grief.

Walking the grief journey with God takes on an active role in our lives. As everything with God, we must engage him. He doesn't force himself upon us or demand that we grieve—he willingly opens his arms to engage us.

Engagement that looks like:

- Thinking
- Learning
- Crying
- Talking
- Praying

- Journaling
- Questioning
- Sharing
- Emoting
- Persisting

Perhaps this list overwhelms you and you are tempted to give up and quit. Try a few of them—journal and pray, question and share, or learn and emote more—but always persist.

CONCLUSION

The grief journey is perhaps our toughest journey we'll ever experience. Other challenges may seem minor in comparison. This however, is not a challenge we've sought—grief is thrust upon us and often when we are least prepared. Into this arena, God steps in. His heart of compassion shows up when most needed. He intimately touches and heals our innermost needs. His loving hand restores us to solace, sanity, and relief.

God allows us (even beckons us) to approach him as he draws close—it is a dance of sorts. We struggle, ask questions, experience new and raw emotions, and often feel quite distant from God. God listens and cares. In faith we engage him, knowing he eagerly calls out and waits for our engagement. God responds to us with an unexpected compassion and understanding. Take this opportunity to find an empathic, loving and kind God—perhaps One you've never experienced before.

END NOTES

[1] Lewis, C.S. *A Grief Observed*. HarperCollins Publishers, 1961.

[2] *The Grief Recovery Handbook 20th Anniversary Expanded Edition: The Action Program for Moving Beyond Death, Divorce, and Other Losses including Health, Career, and Faith*, Russell Friedman and John James

[3] Craig Lounsbrough is a highly regarded counselor and author of several Christian books.

Digging Deeper

Think about the day you heard the news of the passing of your loved one.
What was that day like for you? _____

_____

_____

What was the first thing you said? _____

_____

What emotions did you feel? _____

_____

_____

What verse in Psalm 31 means the most to you and why? _____

_____

_____

We typically feel many different emotions or think a variety of thoughts toward God upon the loss of a loved one. Share some of your emotions and
thoughts in the weeks after your loved one passed. _____

_____

_____

How has your grief drawn you closer to or more distant from God?

_____

_____

What unanswered questions do you have for God concerning your loss? ___

_____

_____

I am the Lord. The One that takes your right hand and says to you,
"don't be afraid, I will help you." —Isaiah 41:13

JOURNALING

JOURNALING

CHAPTER THREE

WE REACH OUT: OUR FRIENDS, FAMILY, AND GRIEF

> *You have taken from me my closest friends and have made me repulsive to them. I am confined and cannot escape; my eyes are dim with grief.*
> —Psalm 88:8-9

I love the Lord's church—the good, the bad, and the ugly. It is the perfect place for the griever. Close, involved friendships, and spiritual insight abound. The church can be an encouraging, engaging, and effective social setting for our grief journey. Often a listening ear can be found as well. I love the church and am grateful for having this group of believers to mourn with.

But, as in all areas of life, Christians are not perfect. We say ridiculous things to try and help those in grief—or we say nothing at all. Sometimes we try to "fix" grief or suggest after a week of mourning, it's time to move on. In a good-hearted effort to help, we might actually hurt others. This is an area where we simply need good information and this chapter provides that.

Remember the disciples with Jesus, Moses, and Elijah in Luke 9 up on the Mount of Transfiguration? The scene was fraught with intensity, intrigue, and mystery, so it was probably a good time to simply watch, listen, and look for Jesus to take the lead. But our good friend Peter jumped in with a dubious comment.

> *As the men were leaving Jesus, Peter said to him, "Master, it is good for us to be here. Let us put up three shelters—one for you, one for Moses and one for Elijah." (He did not know what he was saying.) While he was speaking, a cloud appeared and covered them, and they were afraid as they entered the cloud. A voice came from the cloud, saying, "this is my Son, whom I have chosen; listen to him."*
> —Luke 9:33-35

As a leader, Peter thought he needed to say something and so he spoke. He didn't make much sense, but he spoke. The Scriptures state that, "he did not know what he was saying"—sometimes we should just bite our tongues. People say things like, "Hey, at least your mom was around to see her grandkids" or "Try to think of nice things" or "It's time to move on." We say things to say things. God had to remind Peter of an essential feature of compassionate communication—listen!

Listening is essential to help the griever. Listening with a humble heart and a patient spirit is crucial, if we want to help. Everyone is better off when we listen in difficult times, rather than so easily defaulting to fix-it mode by offering our unsolicited advice. Refuse the temptation to say something just to fill space. Learn to be OK with some silence, or ask a question that elicits more conversation from the griever. Sometimes we should sit in silence, as a "present" friend. For more on this, see Appendix A, "Helping the Hurting," or review "Learning to Hold the Moment" in Chapter 1.

Sometimes we just don't know what to say. We feel the need to say something so we say things that are not helpful, untrue, or downright damaging.

Remember, grief is an issue of a broken heart, not so much a problem with our thinking. Our friends and family can say things that may be rational and intellectually true but emotionally desolate. The words someone uses in an attempt to heal may ring hollow and be detrimental to the griever's soul.

Think about Job's struggle. Everything had been taken away from him—his children, his possessions, his job, and his health—virtually everything. Life had gotten so difficult for Job that he took a broken piece of pottery to scrape sores on his body while his wife said, *"curse God and die"* (Job 2:8-9). It was one tough grief journey for Job.

Job's friends were trying to explain and justify his losses with all sorts of rationale. They said it must have been his fault; he must have done something to anger God. They commented that perhaps God was extremely mad at Job, and everything that was happening to him was some kind of divine payback. Let's look at Job and his friends and some of the ways they tried to help him in his grief. Have you ever said these words (or thought them)? I have.

> *Then Job replied: "How long will you torment me and crush me with words?*
> —Job 19:1-2

WORDS AND STATEMENTS PEOPLE MAY USE[2]:

- **They say nothing.** Our friends may feel like they are intruding on our grief and simply avoid the topic. How does the griever deal with their friend's silence? Honesty is usually the best approach.

I've found it helpful with my friends to initiate a discussion on my grief struggles by simply saying, "This has been a hard week for me. Can I tell you about it?" or "I'm missing my mom a lot today. Can I tell you a bit about her?" It's generally good to talk about death and its impact on you with your friends. I always appreciate someone asking me to tell them about my parents.

- **"You were lucky to have had them all these years."** I suppose this has some truth to it. I am fortunate to have my mom for 50 years—she was loving, kind, and a wonderful mom. But saying this is somehow supposed to makes the loss hurt less? What is the magic number of years where grief will not be present when we lose someone? Twenty years? Thirty? Forty? Fifty? This comment does not help. It's as if there is a set number of years, after which we need to not feel the pain of a loss. I knew my mom for 50 years, but the pain of losing her was huge and has at times been overwhelming. Trying to mitigate one's loss does not help.

- **"You should be over this"** or **"It's time to move on."** Well, that's easy for someone else to say, especially since they aren't the one grieving. These kinds of statements indicate that there is a set way and timeline in which to deal with grief—which we know is not true. We all grieve in different ways, at different times, and for different lengths of time. Grief can sometimes be a complex phenomenon that can be relentless in its ability to hurt and distract.

Trying to push a time agenda on others is not only insensitive but also not helpful. If you are concerned about the length of time one has been in grief, try to learn more about their journey. What else is going on in their life? Are there other struggles present? Are there relationship challenges among friends and family? Work to be present with your grieving friend. Ask questions about their experience, their loved one, and how you might be able to help.

- **"Don't feel bad"** or **"Your loved one wouldn't want you to cry."** This reaction adds to the guilt someone may already be feeling. It implies that somehow someone's emotional display is wrong. This statement usually reflects the discomfort of friends as they try to comfort the griever. Again, honesty is usually the proper response. The griever should courageously allow his or her feelings to simply be what they are.

I know that this can be quite uncomfortable and scary for the griever and denying one's emotions may serve a shorter-term purpose. But God gives emotions to us for a purpose and we shouldn't stuff them but rather fully engage them.

Crying is not only cathartic, it draws others to us. With our emotions on display we get more connected, become less isolated, and are able to engage our grief journey in a more appropriate way. Crying is not only cathartic but draws others to us. With our emotions on display we get more connected, become less isolated and are able to engage our grief journey in a more helpful and appropriate way.

My brother, Danny, and I had times over the phone after the memorial service for my mom, during which we shared stories and tears as we processed our loss. We felt no shame in doing so, and it only served to draw us closer even though we live 2,000 miles apart. *We honor our loved ones by authentically expressing our emotions, not hiding them.*

- **"I know how you feel."** While this is often said with a good heart by someone wanting to help—it usually doesn't. For two reasons: first, it takes the attention off the griever and puts it on the helper. All of a sudden it becomes about them. They've managed to hijack the conversation without even realizing it. Secondly, the helper doesn't know exactly how the griever feels. Other people didn't know my mom for the 50 plus years like I did; they don't have the shared history—good and bad—I had with my mom. This statement assumes all grief is the same, which we know to be false.

- **"Time heals all wounds."** No, it doesn't—time can only delay the need to work through the grief, push the hurt down further, or numb someone to the wound found in grief. Time, combined with work on the grief journey brings healing.

- **"I know you're hurting, but the pain you're subjecting yourself to is doing more harm than good."** For healing to take place we must lean into the pain, not run away from it. Only time combined with walking the grief journey brings about healing.

- **"Your loss reminds me of when my dog died."** Not only is this hijacking the conversation—taking the attention off the griever and putting it on the helper—but a grasping-at-straws attempt to relate. Such a comment minimizes the griever's pain by relating his or her loss to someone or something else. Instead, ask questions, offer words of comfort, or listen and hug.

- **"Well, they're in a better (or worse) place."** Our friends may intellectualize loss or become theologians, and comments of this nature can be offensive and compound someone's grief. These comments are perhaps the most offensive. How do we know what God is doing? Are we now playing God? Have we studied the Bible so thoroughly that we're ready to apply these truths to people we don't know?

These types of comments may produce immense pain during the grief journey. Not only are these comments not helpful, and often quite harmful, but they are simply not appropriate for the needs of the griever. Remember, even Job allowed God space to take care of some of the most difficult matters.

> *Then Job replied to the LORD: "I know that you can do all things; no purpose of yours can be thwarted. You asked, 'Who is this that obscures my plans without knowledge?' Surely I spoke of things I did not understand, things too wonderful for me to know.* —Job 42:3

I've found that many Christians try to frame their loss around the concept of whether or not their loved one was a Christian. This is not helpful for most and usually adds confusion to one's grief journey. Instead, strive to be a compassionate listener for your friend.

The issue here is that you lost a loved one and the relationship that you had for many years. The real work of grief is the restoration and honoring of a lost relationship. Your loved one had a responsibility to know God. I have not found it helpful to rehash "what I could have done" or the "if onlys" of life. Spend your energies on grieving the loss in the relationship and not judging [a lost loved one's] salvation. Judging someone is God's job.

Listening is essential to help the griever. Listening with a humble heart and a patient spirit is best when times get difficult and you want to "fix" your friend. *Refuse the temptation to say something just to fill space. Learn to be OK with some silence.*

MOURNING: THE SOCIAL SIDE OF GRIEF

In Denver, we often had our grief group just before the evening church service. While it was often a time of raw emotions, it also taught us that we engage grief among our closest friends. One thing I love about being a part of the grief group is that these are friends who have faced the most difficult dramas in life and are still standing and ready to engage life. Real people, real issues, real love and real life.

Many are puzzled about the difference between grief and mourning. We can confuse the two, but there is an important difference. Grief is inside of us; it is how we deal with death internally through our emotions, heart, and mind. Grief encompasses sadness, anger, fear, relief, and love. All of us grieve internally over our losses. Our grief may last for days, weeks, months, or even years. Grief tends to be more personal in nature.

Mourning is grief expressed in a community setting. Mourning is social in nature—that is, how we live out our grief. This is where many of us find our losses difficult to deal with. We're OK with grief behind closed doors but many are unwilling to live it out with our family and friends.

God made us as social beings. As Christians, we live out much of our lives socially in the church. Check out the numerous "one another" passages in the Bible. We were created to live life among others—why would we want to do this journey on our own? There is a special connection that comes about from embarking on a grief journey with others.

Mourning reveals an American inconsistency. The society tells us we shouldn't deal with grief publicly and often, even in the church, we practice this. We're surrounded by loss and death and will often spend a lot of money on a funeral or memorial service. Still, life goes on. We are without a loved one and life is changed forever. Let's look at the incredible opportunity God has given us in friends and family.

FOUR FRIENDS

Remember the four friends in Mark who helped their friend up on the roof to get to Jesus, because they could not get in the front door? They lowered their friend through the roof and Jesus healed the man because, "he saw their faith"—all five of them. We often need a few faithful friends to help us along our way on our grief journey.

At our Disciples In Motion[2] groups (for those finding recovery from addictions, relationship problems, and other issues) we've given these four friends names: Relater, Friend, Listener, and Truth-Teller. See if this proves helpful, as you consider your friends helping you in your grief journey.

Relater: This is a fellow mourner who has walked this trail before. They know how to relate to your experiences without judging you and trying to tell you "where you should be by now." He or she might be your most valuable ally, especially as we experience our first major loss in life. The Relater can help by communicating some of the features of their grief journey and how they navigated the waters. Knowing that the journey is unique for everyone, there are still commonalities that many find useful to know.

How the Relater Helps: On the day after an intense "grief dream" (see chapter 5) about my mother, I was feeling the same raw feeling as the day she died. I feared that this might be a long-lasting emotion and this caused me great concern. I called my good friend Mark Young, who had pioneered the way of grief for me, and he assured me that the raw feelings pass eventually. He reminded me that the first year has some challenges— anniversaries, birthdays, and holidays, but that things get better. A Relater is invaluable.

Friend: I've noticed over the years in the school setting that I work in that kids in grief often find school to be the one safe place where life is normal. They get to do normal things and temporarily forget about the chaos of grief at home. We too need times with friends to simply enjoy life and not be on the grief trail for a time. We need safe friends who know how to care for us by just being a friend. You often may need to "teach" your friend how to help by asking for time together, etc. Take charge of your recovery and find a friend.

How the Friend Helps: This is the person who is there to help make life normal again. A friend is someone to go out for a coffee or beer with, to see a movie or sporting event with, to go on a hike or exercise with. A friend does something to remind the griever that life continues and will eventually return to normal. A friend knows when this is appropriate and may have to make the initial move to help the griever find some sense of normalcy.

Listener: This is someone to listen without having all the answers. We all have the need to talk and get the pain, challenges, nuances of grief and life events off our chest. This person can be hard to find. Many people are not good at listening and they may quickly cut in and try to "relate."

One trick that has worked for me is to tell a good friend that I'll buy dinner if they listen and only listen—and then I talk. When they interrupt to "relate" or advise, I remind them that I bought dinner so I get to talk. Being able to talk at length with a confidant is inexpensive yet effective therapy. Simply being able to sit with someone in their grief and being present with them can be invaluable for the griever. Even crying with someone who is grieving can do wonders for them.

How the Listener Helps: They listen without judgment. They listen for long periods of time. They know how to gently ask relevant questions that elicit more conversation. A good listener who generally withholds advice and information until appropriate is a rare find. The griever walks away with a sense of having been heard. Offering a listening ear and validation to those in grief is vital.

Truth-Teller: Sometimes we stray and get off the trail. Perhaps we find ourselves lashing out at others and justifying ourselves because we are grieving. Or we eat too much comfort food and gain weight. Or an addiction has returned, and we need someone to gently guide us back—we need a Truth-Teller.

How the Truth-Teller Helps: Grievers are prone to becoming emotionally distraught and may lose their footing in important areas of life. They may make decisions in the heat of the moment that will have long-term negative consequences or fall back into destructive and addictive behaviors. At times, grievers need a Truth-Teller.

This is a special role and must be handled with gentleness, wisdom, and compassion. I will often preface a truth comment by saying, "May I suggest?" or "I have a thought. Do you mind if I share it?" I will have pondered a scripture in advance or sought advice from a trusted friend to help guide me. Also, I try to carve out the time to finish the talk and not leave my friend hanging.

It's rare for us to find all these characteristics in one person, so I encourage you to find different friends that meet different needs. Pray through your friendships and ask the friends you know for help. See Appendix A: Helping The Hurting Friend for more on how to help those in grief.

FAMILY

Grief can cause intense strain on your family, regardless of how close you may have been before the loss. Childhood issues may resurface or lifelong hurts and sins may rear their ugly heads. Or mistrust may be present as the estate is settled. God placed you within a family for you to love and support one another. He does not want you to squabble over issues during this time. It is OK to express your differences, but personal attacks and hurtful accusations are always out of line. Your family should be a safe place where love is the context in which disagreements are worked out.

Grief is time for the family to pull together and lean on each other for strength. Pray for unity. Stay humble. Practice patience and grace. Don't make a difficult situation even more challenging.

Death can bring about an incredibly emotional closeness never before experienced in a family. I experienced this after my mom passed. My oldest brother, Chris, who I had grown up somewhat intimidated of, turned out to be my hero in the difficult days after my mom died. When I arrived at the home for the memorial service, he quickly took me under his wing and brought me up to speed on everything—who was in the house, what the plans were for the service, how he was doing, etc. Because of his humor, vulnerability, and caring leadership our family has grown immensely in our love for each other.

CONCLUSION

We have to push back against society's opinions about grief (feel little, say little, love little, just move on, and quickly get over our grief) as well our natural impulse to ignore our own grief; instead, we need to engage the community of fellow grievers as well as those who wish to help.

Mourning is our grief in a social context. It is also living our grief among friends and family—those who know us best and care for us the most. As grievers, we need community more than ever. Others may not always say the right things at the right times and sometimes may even harm us with their words, but they are infinitely better than facing our grief alone.

When we honestly ask ourselves which person in our lives means the most to us, we often find that it is those who, instead of giving advice, solutions, or cures, have chosen rather to share our pain and touch our wounds with a warm and tender hand. The friend who can be silent with us in a moment of despair or confusion, who can stay with us in an hour of grief and bereavement, who can tolerate not knowing, not curing, not healing and face with us the reality of our powerlessness, that is a friend who cares. —Henri Nouwen

---

END NOTES

[1] Friedman & James. *The Grief Recovery Handbook, 20th Anniversary Expanded Edition: The Action Program for Moving Beyond Death, Divorce, and Other Losses including Health, Career, and Faith*, HarperCollins Publishers, 2009.

[2] Disciples In Motion is a unique and innovative church-based recovery ministry. Dr. Sumerlin and his wife, Jackie developed this ministry in 2011 and it is currently operating in Denver, as well as the Dallas-Ft. Worth Church and the Los Angeles Church of Christ. For more information go to www.inmotioncounseling.org.

Digging Deeper

What myths about grief have you previously believed? _____

_____

_____

_____

What are some statements that others may have made to you that did not prove helpful?" _____

_____

_____

_____

_____

_____

What is the most helpful statement you heard? _____

_____

_____

_____

_____

Review the "four friends" from this chapter. Is there an area you lack in your friendships? _____

_____

_____

_____

_____

Two are better than one, because they have a good return for their labor:
If either of them falls down, one can help the other up.
But pity anyone who falls and has no one to help them up.
—Ecclesiastes 4: 9-10

JOURNALING _____

_____

_____

_____

_____

_____

_____

_____

_____

_____

_____

_____

_____

_____

_____

_____

_____

_____

_____

_____

_____

_____

_____

_____

_____

JOURNALING _____

_____

_____

_____

_____

_____

_____

_____

_____

_____

_____

_____

_____

_____

_____

_____

_____

_____

_____

_____

_____

_____

_____

_____

_____

_____

_____

JOURNALING

_____

_____

_____

_____

_____

_____

_____

_____

_____

_____

_____

_____

_____

_____

_____

_____

_____

_____

_____

_____

_____

_____

_____

_____

CHAPTER FOUR

YOUR GRIEF NARRATIVE: A LIFETIME OF LOSS

They will soar on wings like eagles; they will run and not grow weary, they will walk and not be faint. —Isaiah 40:31

Heathcliff was my favorite dog, companion, and best friend. Heathcliff had run away before, but we always found him quickly. This time was different, as "Heathy" had been missing for several days. I had a feeling of foreboding in my gut that all would not end well for me and Heathy.

My dad and I went out on a Sunday afternoon looking for Heathcliff. About a block from our home we found him lying dead alongside a busy road. I was devastated and cried my eyes out. After bringing him home, no one in my family spoke of his death—it was like it never happened.

The next day at school I wandered around aimlessly. It seemed like my world had fallen apart, and I would just have to learn how to deal with it by myself. So, I hid. Hid my emotions, hid my fears, and even tried to hide my tears. It was the first real loss in my life and it wouldn't be the last.

Through the years, the losses seemed to pile up: my Aunt Ceil, Aunt Myrtle, grandpas and grandmas. There have been students of mine (I work as a professional counselor) who have died due to suicide, illnesses, drug overdoses, and accidents. My best friend committed suicide. I lost a friend to a brain tumor and others perished in car wrecks. There were pets that died, miscarriages, and the children of friends who died. But the most devastating losses for me have been the deaths of my mother and father.

I learned to take loss in stride—don't feel it too deeply, just move on and hide. Grieving loss meant weakness and there was too much work to do to be weak. For me, hiding took less energy than engaging my grief.

My parents' passing halted this ignorance of grief. I was no longer able to overlook my grief—it had to be paid attention to and processed. I found it to be "dishonoring" to ignore my parents' passing and "just move on." Somehow, I needed to pause long enough to fully engage my grief. In 2007, I began a journey to do so.

One exercise I have found to be very helpful is creating a lifetime grief narrative[1] —a thorough, cumulative chronicling of the losses in my life, my initial responses to each, and how some continue to influence me today. Without understanding the many losses in my life, I was unsure about how to move on. I was shocked at the variety and number of deaths that had accumulated over the years in my life. I was also perplexed at the ways I had learned to handle my losses. Finally, I was surprised at the way grief had pulled on me mentally, emotionally, physically, and spiritually.

At the end of this chapter, you have the opportunity to write a narrative of your lifetime of significant losses and how each one has impacted you. The number of people, relationships, pets, jobs, and other losses you've endured may astonish you.

One reason grief disrupts so many aspects of our life is because our loss is not one isolated loss, but losses piled upon losses. Without spending some time on a grief journey, we fail to reconnect with and be reminded of the amazing qualities family and friends we've lost, and how blessed we were by their presence. Each loss becomes an opportunity to experience grief.

Since grief comes to everyone why do some people seem to work through it better than others? Dr. H. Norman Wright says this about lifelong loss: "Some people think that going through the losses or crises of life are the exceptional times, I see it differently. I see the times of calm as the exceptions. Life really is going through one loss after another, one crisis after another."

Instead of avoiding talking about these times, let's do our homework. When you know what to expect, you're not thrown by them as much, and you're going to be better able to recover."

A few thoughts about a lifetime of loss:

Although countless people have experienced grief before you, each person's response to grief is different. The way you deal with a lifetime of loss will be uniquely your own. Be careful how you view your lifelong grief issues in light of others' opinions. Our experiences are different from others because we view the world through a different lens: our history, personality, emotional make-up, and socio-economic status differs from those of other people.

Loss and the grief associated with it, if unprocessed, can have a profound outcome on our family dynamics, personality, friendships, self-esteem, and even our dreams for the future.

Taking some time in the **Digging Deeper** exercise at the end of the chapter may reap huge dividends. Don't skip over this opportunity as you may find some rich nuggets of insight into your personal make-up and worldview.

You have a new and changed identity. Perhaps your losses have created a different "you." What piece of your identity has been lost or gained? Was your loved one your friend, lover, encourager, or the family comedian? Perhaps they were the bread winner or a trusted friend. Maybe they were your shoulder to cry on, the arms that hugged and comforted you, or your greatest cheerleader in life. Their passing probably changed you in some lasting way.

It is vital to acknowledge this change. When someone close to us dies, a part of us dies with them. When I lost my parents, I lost a foundation of security and for the first time in my life was totally on my own. This was not necessarily a bad thing—just something I needed to acknowledge, accept, and adjust to.

You may take on different degrees of change in regards to your identity to accommodate your loss. Perhaps there are new realities in your life to acknowledge that you've not yet considered. This is where we often feel stuck as we vacillate between the old and the new realities of life. Maybe you're living in an old paradigm that is confusing because you've not yet accepted your new role. Are there new responsibilities for you in your life, or perhaps you're undergoing an identity crises of sorts? Try verbalizing how your personality has changed—good and bad—to God.

Your list may be any number of identities. Say them out loud to God—he knows your intricate identity and he alone can reinvent you.

Consider and complete the following questions:

When I had significant loss, my identity was changed in these ways: _____

_____

My new identity includes: _____

_____

_____

IDENTITY

Remember that your true spiritual identity is rooted in Christ. As Christians, we no longer place all of our identity in our physical lives, our history, labels given to us, or in our sins and character faults, but in Christ. We rely on what the Bible teaches us about our identity. While much about our positive and current identity may prove helpful and affirming, the true identity we hold is that of being "in Christ." Here are a few reminders found in the Scriptures about our identity in Christ: we are called new creations, adopted sons, part of a royal priesthood, holy nation, treasured possessions, living stones, brothers, sisters, and friends of Jesus.

God sees us as redeemed, lights, lamps, citizens of a city on a hill, and shining stars. He tells us that he has an etching on his hand with our name on it. These names (and dozens more in the Bible) are God's identifying monikers for each of us as Christians—this is how he sees us. You should do the same.

> The LORD will fulfill [his purpose] for me; your love, O LORD, endures forever—do not abandon the works of your hands. —Psalm 138:8

CREATING HOPE

> Remember, O God, that my life is but a breath; my eyes will never see happiness again" —Job 7:7

Will life always feel this way? Will I get over my loss? Will it always feel this raw? Job had similar questions and feelings. Job thought he would "never see happiness again," as he suffered loss upon loss. Would loss be the sum of his life? Or would Job find a different outcome? Most of us at times feel like our life is over, that somehow, we're "done" and this grief we're experiencing will be a lifetime ally, never to be discarded. But when we read the end of the book of Job, we find that God had something very good in store for him (Job 42:12).

The first year after your loss is often the most difficult, as anniversaries, birthdays, holidays, and other reminders crop up. Being aware of these events and planning for them can be helpful. There are many creative ways (Google "creative ways to plan grief anniversaries") to acknowledge, memorialize, and honor the different anniversaries of your loved ones. Acknowledge, embrace, and engage these special dates and find ways to honor, instead of ignoring these times. You will find more on this in chapter 7.

Life will not always feel raw—you will adjust. But life will never be the same either. In our grief, many of us sometimes feel like our life is over, that somehow the grief we're experiencing will dog us for the rest of our life and we'll never be the same. Much of this adjustment may depend on how you frame your loss.

Framing loss: Just as a good frame makes a picture "perfect," we frame events in our lives. How we view our circumstances and losses often reveals how we see life unfold before us and how we place ourselves, our loved ones, and God in those events.

Of course, when things go well—a new relationship, a raise, or recent degree—we frame our worldview around a good and loving God who cares for us. Look at what God did: He answered our prayers, our work paid off, or we simply smile at the goodness of life.

On the other hand, when times get rough—we lose a job, friendships go sour, or we suffer the loss of a loved one—we may begin to doubt God's goodness. We may begin to frame our losses around ideas like, "Why is God doing this to me?" or "I don't deserve this," or the popular go-to, "Life just stinks."

The manner in which we view or frame our losses can be monumental in how we move through our grief journey. As William Arthur Ward famously said, "The pessimist complains about the wind; the optimist expects it to change; the realist adjusts the sails."

We can't always predict the future, change the outcomes, or make life happen the way we want, but we always have the opportunity and power to react to life's unfolding drama. We make choices every day on how much and in what direction to adjust our sails.

Consider the following thought from Craig Lounsbrough in *An Autumn's Journey: Deep Growth in the Grief and Loss of Life's Seasons:*

> *"Is loss really loss, or is it the pinnacle of God's work in a person's life much like fall? In a life well lived, is it really nothing more than an acknowledgement that the final touches have been made; that the person has been fully painted with the brushes of perfection? At these moments, would it not make sense that anything else, any addition despite how small would only bring diminishment? Is it reasonable to believe that it's now time to frame that person or that situation with the timelessness of eternity, handing whatever it is over to God?"*

END NOTES

[1] Caplan & Lang. *Grief's Courageous Journey: A Workbook.* New Harbinger Publications, Oakland, CA, 1996.

Digging Deeper

We experience loss through a lifetime. Ponder the losses you've lived through. Think about the losses and any themes you see they created in your life and jot down notes related to your losses.

Include losses in the "Experienced Loss" section that influenced you during the different stages of life. These may include pets, relationships, dreams, abuses and of course, the loss of loved ones. There are other losses such as a loss of innocence due to abuse, the loss of a cherished possession, or the devastation of losing everything in a fire or other disaster, moving away, changes in career or school, divorce, plus anything you consider to be a significant loss.

As you write down your losses, think about the themes that you may have developed to deal with your losses. These themes may include areas such as anger, loneliness, fear, isolation, substance abuse, sexual promiscuity, and the like. Try to be as vulnerable and honest as you can be and remember to keep this journal in a safe place.

Add additional thoughts in the "Notes" section.

Don't compare yourself to others and then attempt to minimize your losses.2 We all have a variety of losses that are different than those experiences of others and impact us in different ways. Often, we want to compare our losses to those of others and then degrade our own loss—I find this most unhelpful. My losses are vastly different from yours (and yours' from mine) and we can each own our losses. It's OK to acknowledge and accept any losses you've experienced and simply allow them to be what they are.

An example on my Lifetime Loss chart, under the Ages 1-12 section I wrote:

- In the "Experienced Loss" section, I wrote: "In 5th grade, my dog, Heathcliff, died by being run over by a car."

- In the "Theme" section, I wrote: "Because no one talked about this, it caused me to believe it is not OK to publicly grieve so I hid."

- In the "Notes" section I wrote: "After 48 years, it still hurts a bit. Early negative lesson in grief."

Simply take each loss for what it is and honor it for what you've experienced in it.

Fill in graph on pages 72-73 and answer these questions:

What surprised you about your lifetime losses? _____

_____

_____

Which losses feel the worst? _____

_____

_____

How did you respond to your losses? List themes here:_____

_____

_____

What one overall theme do you notice? _____

_____

_____

How have your losses shaped your personality? _____

_____

_____

_____

Do you tend to run away and ignore grief or embrace it? How do you
know? _____

_____

_____

My most significant loss is (the one that hurts the most now—often the
reason you came to this group): _____

_____

_____

STAGES	EXPERIENCED LOSS
Ages 1-12	
As a teenager	
Young adult	
As a parent	
As an older adult	

THEME AS A RESULT OF THE LOSS	NOTES
Ages 1-12	
As a teenager	
Young adult	
As a parent	
As an older adult	

JOURNALING

JOURNALING

CHAPTER FIVE

PERSONAL GRIEF: WHY DOES THIS HURT SO MUCH?

> *"I am weary with my sighing; Every night I make my bed swim, I dissolve my couch with my tears. My eye has wasted away with grief"*—Psalm 6:6-7 (NASB)

It was a few weeks after my mom's memorial service when I was back in Denver and life was moving on, slowly, and somewhat painfully. Early one Sunday morning I had a dream—not just any dream, but a dream I'll never forget. A dream I would not sell for a million dollars. A dream about my mom and me.

> *In the dream, we were standing in a spot in her house between the kitchen and dining room—a place we had often talked. She appeared normal, even cheerful, and we spoke for a few moments. She told me, "I'm OK" and "Don't worry." In the dream I began to cry and then she did something she often did when emotions appeared in our home – she "schussed" me—used her hands to indicate that emotions were not welcome here. This was something she did when things got uncomfortable emotionally. We hugged and then she left.*

I woke up and sat on the edge of my bed, shaken. It felt so real, I could almost feel and smell her. I longed to get the dream back and experience her presence once more. Then the thought occurred to me to just forget the dream and move on—time to get ready for church and a busy day. It was just a dream.

But then I thought of my mom and all that she meant to me and, how by "moving on," I would dishonor her and her memory. As I sat on my bed I began to weep, and I decided then and there to fully engage my mom's passing and the dream I had about her. That raw feeling of the day she passed returned, but I had made the right choice—the choice to fully engage.

Some say dreams are just a scattering of fragments getting reorganized and erased during our sleep, like a hard drive defragmenting. Others go as far as to say dreams are actual events in a spiritual world. I have my own thoughts. The Bible also has something to say about dreams.

Dreams are found 104 times in the Bible. Heroes like Jacob, Joseph, Gideon, Solomon, Samuel, Daniel and Job dreamed. Joseph (Jesus' dad) dreamed about Jesus and how to keep him safe. There are dreams that spoke of the future, reminders of the past, to emphasize a truth, or dreams that scare us. Some dreams may demonstrate the good and right things of God and some dreams tell us evil things, not of God. You will need to decide for yourself to place whatever value you find in your dreams. (See Appendix F for more insight on grief dreams.)

The point here is that we all process grief in very personal terms and in unique ways. Some of us dream. Others write. Some process grief by not changing a single thing about their lives. I've known several people who returned to destructive habits to deal with their grief. Some make major life decisions (one friend of mine, right after losing a parent, moved his family out into the mountains—a lifetime goal of his—most researchers agree that it may not be wise to make major life choices immediately after a loss). Still others, talk to process grief. How about you? How do you process your grief?

PERSONALLY DEALING WITH GRIEF

We all deal with grief; some stuff their feelings and file away their loss in the farthest recesses of their mind; others, engage, talk about and process their grief. Perhaps, in an effort to escape the pain, we may sometimes look for short-term solutions such as a former addiction or a habit like isolation, overeating, massive social media involvement, overworking, alcohol, drugs, or smoking. These destructive choices have two elements in common: they prolong the actual grieving process and add negatively to the complexity of our journey.

Thankfully, no one told me how I should feel during this time—most of my friends simply listened and loved. Never allow anyone to tell you how you should feel. All grief is individual, personal, and dependent upon the unique and historical relationship we had with our loved one. Obviously, the longer we knew someone, the more they influenced our lives, and the closer we were will determine the level and intricacies of the grief we experience.

One truth is that we all deal with our grief. This chapter will explore some of those ways and how we might more effectively deal with our grief.

NORMAL EXPECTATIONS OF THE GRIEF JOURNEY

These are not common for everyone, every time, but do seem to show up often:

- You will need to mourn and grieve with intention and dedicate time to do so.

- There seem to be no absolutes or stages to go through. Instead, grief is individual and relationship specific. We do need time and space to properly grieve.

- You will most likely experience many different thoughts and feelings, some positive, some negative. Most emotions are value neutral so, try not to place a moral value on them—just acknowledge them for what they are and what message they bring. Emotions can be quite unpredictable so carefully navigate those waters with a friend, family, and the Word as your guide.

Your grief will impact all five areas of your life—mental, physical, emotional, spiritual and social. Pay attention to all five.

- **Mental:** You may experience confusion, distraction, appear preoccupied and unfocused. Concentration and mental acuity may suffer.

- **Physical:** You may sleep more than normal or have trouble sleeping. Some will over or under eat and may lack the motivation to exercise.

- **Emotional:** A wide range of emotions are possible and expected.

- **Spiritual:** Questions about God and your purpose in life may occur. You may find yourself praying more or less than usual. Some experience a distance from God and others see their attendance at church decrease.

- **Socially:** You may withdraw from friends or narrow your choice of friends. This is common, as you often need more energy to spend in the grieving process. Others may become clingy and have an unhealthy dependence on others.

GRIEVING AS UNIQUE INDIVIDUALS

As individuals, we grieve in many different ways. Phrases like, "you should be over this by now" or "haven't you spent enough time grieving?" are particularly hurtful to the griever. Why? Because we are all unique individuals and we all grieve in unique ways with a variety of timelines and features to our grief. Why are we different from others in our grief journey? Here are three reasons why:

1. Simply put, God made us different from each other. Paul states in

Ephesians 2:9, "For we are God's workmanship" The Greek word for workmanship is *"poetrea"* from where we get the English word, "poetry." God says we were created and live as poetry, as if each of us were made with different words, tone, verses, pitch, and rhythm to life. Since we were created differently, we grieve differently.

2. We each have a diverse spiritual, physical, emotional, social and mental makeup. We come to grieving with different strengths and weaknesses as well as a distinctive set of coping skills. Our first time grieving a significant loss may look different from our second, third or fourth.

3. We each have a special relationship with our loved ones who died. We have lived a vastly different set of historical, socio-emotional and intricate relationships that we grieve. There is absolutely no way that we can grieve like the rest—even if we tried!

All grief is individual, personal and typically dependent upon the unique and historical relationship we had with our loved one.

CIRCUMSTANCES THAT MAY AFFECT OUR GRIEF

When, how and where death occurs, may produce different responses from us. For instance, when my father passed, I was more prepared having grieved my mother's passing four years earlier. Here are a few ideas concerning the circumstances that influence our grief:

- **Your relationship with the person who died.** The stronger the attachment to your loved one, the more difficult your grief journey may be. Also, the greater the area you liked least about that person, the more you may struggle. Considering their personality, how they thought of you and how they influenced your life may complicate the grieving.

- **Circumstances of their death.** Was their death sudden? Were you prepared? Most of us are never really "prepared" even if we know of an imminent death but sudden death has unique challenges. Sometimes controversy complicates.

- **Your own history of grief, mourning and death issues.** See chapter 4.

- **Current stressors in your life.** Other current losses such as a job loss, divorce, etc. may influence the severity of your grief for your loved one.

- **Your unique personality.** Your history including your gender, culture, struggles with any addictions and personal strengths and weaknesses figure into how you grieve.

- **What you have already done to deal with the loss.** Planning a memorial service or funeral, praying, time spent with a loved one (if their demise was drawn out), time spent consoling and being consoled by loved ones have an impact on the grieving process.

- **Support systems.** The people you choose to lean while going through the grieving process can prove invaluable or they may leave you unfulfilled.

- **One's faith, hope, love, and trust in God.** People of faith have an edge and can derive comfort in grieving through reading the Bible, prayer, church attendance, and talking with other spiritual people about their loss.

- **Willingness to change.** If we let it, the grieving process can launch us in positive, life-altering ways we never imagined, or it can mire us in the doldrums if we allow it to.

- Remember, God understands and has great compassion on those going through grief. Consider the following words of encouragement from God.

> *Be merciful to me, Lord, for I am in distress; my eyes grow weak with sorrow, my soul and body with grief. My life is consumed by anguish and my years by groaning; my strength fails because of my affliction, and my bones grow weak.*
> —Psalm 31:9-10

Habakkuk encourages you to trust in God and persevere no matter how bad things seem:

> *Though the fig tree does not bud and there are no grapes on the vines, though the olive crop fails and the fields produce no food, though there are no sheep in the pen and no cattle in the stalls, yet will I rejoice in the LORD, I will be joyful in God my Savior. The Sovereign LORD is my strength; he makes my feet like the feet of a deer, he enables me to go on the heights.* —Habakkuk 3:17-19

TAKING CONTROL

God not only gives us strength to endure our grief but to move forward, "he enables me to go on the heights." One of the goals of walking the grief recovery journey with others is that we might take control of our journey and grow, instead of grief controlling us.

A vital decision to make is taking responsibility and control of our hearts. We are ultimately responsible for the direction of our grief journey. While at times, it may feel like grief is "calling the shots," the truth of the matter is that you and I are in control of this time in our lives.

While God moves in mysterious ways and reaches out to direct and mature in us in our walk, we too have free will to make changes and direct how we respond to our grief. We make many decisions each day in our thought life, our behavior, and the direction of our heart.

THE HEART

Above all else, guard your heart —Proverbs 4:23

As you contemplate your response to this challenging time, consider your heart. There are more than 800 references to the heart found in the Bible. Interestingly, roughly 400 refer to a corrupted, evil, or bad heart and about 400 refer to a healthy, growing, or good heart. It seems that we get a choice in the matter.

Consider the following suggestions as you work to overcome some of the heart challenges in your grief journey:

- Keep journaling.
- Look at ways you've changed your heart in the past.
- When needed, ask God for help repenting. (2 Timothy 2:25)
- Remind yourself of the destructive nature of a bad heart.
- Ask the Holy Spirit to change your heart—request this daily in prayer.
- Immerse yourself with the Word—morning, noon, and night.
- Encircle yourself with friends; ask questions and initiate with them.
- Attend *Grief Journey* meetings and listen as others share their hearts.
- Faithfully continue the difficult work of grief recovery.

In John 10:10, Jesus reminds us that he came for us to experience a "full life," that is, to engage and fully embrace life. Please take time to consider your reaction to your loss. Has this loss driven you further away from the full life Jesus promises, or are you more engaged than before?

Remember, "Love always hopes" (I Corinthians 13:7). No matter how difficult things are going today in your grief recovery, the promise from God is that there is always hope. His love guarantees that. Healing can and will occur.

God's Spirit are always at work. Hope often arrives through trusted friends, reconnections made with others, and through your relationship with God.

Take the time this week to consider some of the different ways you've dealt with your grief.

Digging Deeper

What are ways you've responded to grief so far? Include both the good and the unproductive ways you responded to grief. _____

_____

_____

_____

List a few ways you might do more of the good responses. _____

_____

_____

_____

_____

What behaviors in your life have you found to not be effective? _____

_____

_____

_____

How can you take back control of these aberrant behaviors? _____

_____

_____

Who have you talked to about this? _____

"A bend in the road is not the end of the road unless you
fail to make the turn." —Craig Lounsbrough

JOURNALING _____

_____

_____

_____

_____

_____

_____

_____

_____

_____

_____

_____

_____

_____

_____

_____

_____

_____

_____

_____

_____

_____

_____

_____

_____

_____

_____

JOURNALING

CHAPTER SIX

THIS ONE HURTS THE MOST: EXAMINING A RELATIONSHIP

Only people who are capable of loving strongly can also suffer great sorrow,
but this same necessity of loving serves to counteract their grief and heals them.
—Leo Tolstoy

Driving to the Quantico National Military Cemetery in Quantico, Va. with my family was fraught with fear, trepidation, and emotion. As a former lieutenant colonel in the Marine Corps, it was my dad's right to be buried at QNMC, and he and my mom decided that was the place they wanted to be laid to rest; my dad had died six months before and my mom had been gone for more than four years when we had them interred at the QNMC on the same day, together.

An impressive Marine Corps detail had come to perform the ceremony. After delicately carrying the remains to an outdoor portico, the chaplain conducted a thoughtful service, speaking of my parents' devotion to their country and my dad's service in the Corps as an aviator for almost thirty years. The five Sumerlin boys were sitting, oldest to youngest, in the front row, and there wasn't a dry eye to be seen. After the commander presented the flag to my oldest brother Chris, we were rocked in our seats, as a rifle was leveled—seemingly pointed directly at us—and shot after shot rang out as my dad was honored for his years of service with a 21-gun salute. Then a lone Marine, 50 yards away, played "Taps" on his bugle; the moving instrumental echoed throughout the forested hillocks and granite grave markers, ending a fitting ceremony for our beloved parents.

The intensity and formality of the ceremony was comforting to me, as I found my mind race back through mental snapshots of my relationship with my parents. I was reminded of the good times we had together—the unwavering support, years of laughter and fun, a rich familial heritage–as well as difficult times, including disagreements, hurts, and failures. Good times and bad times are common to all relationships.and fun, a rich heritage and the bad times— disagreements, hurts and failures. The good times and the difficult times that are common to all relationships.

HONOR

I find honor in remembering my loved ones. Some refuse to honor their loved ones because of significant faults when alive, but does a person have to be perfect for us to honor them? Do we not honor John F. Kennedy, Martin Luther King, sports figures, and other heroes? Were they perfect? Of course not, but we find their lives worthy of our honor. And so it is with our loved ones. Despite their weaknesses, sins, and mistakes (just like all of us), we find ways to honor them. Just like we appreciate it when we are offered grace during our times of need, we extend grace to those we've lost and honor them.

I've realized honor to be a driving motivation in my grief work. That by honoring those we've lost, we have the ability to carry on our relationship with them. I've come to believe that the life of my loved one carries on inside of me to this day, and my hope is that my life carries on in those I love.

The process of grieving is relationally contextual; that is, the degree of our grief and the process of grieving often depends on the type, texture, duration, and history of the relationship we lost. We may find ourselves grieving little for a distant relative we've had little contact with through the years. Yet, most will grieve tremendously for a parent, especially one who had a positive, lasting impact on our life.

In this chapter, we will explore the relationship that brought us to a grief group or caused us to purchase this book. We'll look at this relationship closely, examining the good and the bad, warts and all, resolving what needs to be resolved, as we write a letter to this missing loved one. Often, we veer in one direction or another—either our loved one was all good or not so good. The majority of relationships, however, are a mix of good times and bad times. We do a disservice to the memory of a loved one by ignoring their faults and mistakes or overemphasizing their good qualities.

Unresolved relationship issues is a recurring theme for most of us, and probably surfaced with our loved one when they were still alive. As I began to work through my grief with my parents, I had to think through the abundance of experiences in our relationship for more than five decades.

There were many great things we enjoyed together, such as food, fun, our educational journeys, family vacations, and the like. They supported my first purchase of a car and when we bought our first home. My parents joyfully attended my wedding and lovingly spent time with my wife and children. They sacrificed many things to help us build our lives. Mom and Dad created a culture in the family of fun, education, service, and grace that I've incorporated into my own family and I now see vestiges of that culture as my children build their own families.

But there were also things that were said between us that produced hurt, such as uncommunicated love, unresolved anger, and misunderstandings. There was gratitude I never fully expressed while my parents were alive—a regret I carry to this day. There are a multitude of emotions and behaviors ascribed to those said or unsaid things.

Take time to dig some of these issues out of the shadows and expose them for what they are. *Often, these are the kinds of barriers that keep us from properly grieving a loss.*

In my own example, I've uncovered lots of emotions, including happiness, sadness, love, fear, anger and compassion, that weren't properly communicated on both sides. We don't need to analyze, compartmentalize, or explain our feelings. We simply need to learn to communicate them effectively so that we can complete any unfinished or undelivered expressive communications.

What about you? What was your relationship like with your loved one? Have you taken the time to fully consider the wide range of lost communications? Perhaps there were good things you've forgotten about, or maybe hurts and pain that still exists and you're stuck.

As I have taken care of the nagging issues between me and my lost loved ones that I'm able to grieve more effectively. Too many of us struggle with grief because we have difficulties in the way, and we can't see past them. This is your opportunity to take some of those barriers off the table, find relief, and experience freedom.

Take some time to consider the full range of your relationship with your loved one. What were the highlights of this relationship? Remember the weddings, birthdays, special times, characteristics that were passed on, lessons learned, gifts given, humor expressed, etc. How about the hard times? Don't avoid recalling the arguments, low points, or unresolved anger. Bring the "whole" of your relationship out.

Digging Deeper

List the five most important events of this relationship:

1)

2)

3)

4)

5)

Every relationship has difficult areas that need to be acknowledged. Taking an honest look at your relationship to your loved one, what areas do you think had a negative affect on you?

1)

2)

3)

4)

5)

How has your loved one influenced your life for the good? What positive characteristics do you have that you might attribute to your loved one?

1)

2)

3)

4)

5)

How did your loved one make you laugh? _____

_____

_____

_____

_____

_____

_____

_____

_____

What will you miss the most in this relationship? _____

_____

_____

_____

_____

_____

_____

_____

_____

What will you miss the least? _____

_____

_____

_____

_____

Summarize your thoughts – what is the spirit or essence of this relationship?

_____

_____

_____

_____

_____

_____

_____

_____

_____

For the next group, you will have an opportunity to share your story with a partner. Each of you will have up to 25 minutes to discuss the Digging Deeper journaling from this chapter, uninterrupted. You may review your journaling, share stories that go along with your journaling, or create a timeline of your relationship with your loved one—whatever you are comfortable with.

This is a special time and often group members find new insights during this time of sharing. After you share, the person who had been in the listening role will take their turn and tell their story.

Storyteller: Share your story for no more than 25 minutes. Remember, this is not a fact-finding mission but a story of the heart, so try not to get bogged down in details but stay with the essence of the story. Take time to pause or cry if needed—this is your time.

Listener: Do not interrupt with questions, comments or touching but simply listen. You may cry, smile or laugh (if appropriate) but do not touch or respond to the storyteller's story. Do your very best to stay "present" with the storyteller, taking in the essence of the story you are hearing. Allow them ample time to pause or cry—this is their time. After they are finished, now you tell your story.

JOURNALING _____

_____

_____

_____

_____

_____

_____

_____

_____

_____

_____

_____

_____

_____

_____

_____

_____

_____

_____

_____

_____

_____

_____

_____

_____

JOURNALING _____

_____

_____

_____

_____

_____

_____

_____

_____

_____

_____

_____

_____

_____

_____

_____

_____

_____

_____

_____

_____

_____

_____

_____

JOURNALING

_____

_____

_____

_____

_____

_____

_____

_____

_____

_____

_____

_____

_____

_____

_____

_____

_____

_____

_____

_____

_____

_____

_____

_____

CHAPTER SEVEN

A GRIEF NARRATIVE: SAYING GOODBYE TO HURT

I found a letter recently that I had written to my two favorite aunts when I was 7 years old. I remember writing it as my mother watched over me—it was painful. The letter was a thank-you note for $1 they had sent me in 1964 for Christmas. The letter apparently meant a lot to them as they placed it in a bible that I found years later, after they had passed. Fifty years later, it's still a treasure.

Letters are a most meaningful means of communication. Letters convey heart, express love and some, last for centuries. John Adams wrote his wife, Abigail, letters that stand to this day and reveal the vibrant history and rich texture of their relationship. Ronald Reagan wrote the nation a letter as he prepared to tackle Alzheimer's disease. Queen Elizabeth, Jane Austin, and Eleanor Roosevelt were prolific letter writers.

Of course, much of the New Testament is made up of letters. Paul, Peter, James, and John spent many hours, led by the Holy Spirit, conveying God's heart for us in narratives—love letters of sorts. I save virtually every correspondence my wife, Jackie, has ever written—every card, every note, and every letter. So, we'll write a letter, a narrative—to our loved one.

YOUR GRIEF NARRATIVE

We don't "get over" our grief as much as we reconcile with it. We learn to live a new life as we've acknowledged our loss, lived with the pain, done everything we can to take away the painful areas of the relationship, and attempt to move forward.

Our hearts have changed, perhaps we see God in a new light and are able to help others. Or we've come to experience the loving hand of God at work in our lives during this most difficult time and for that we are grateful.

This letter-writing time will be a way to wrap up some of this journey—a letter to sum up our thoughts and heart for our loved one. Here are a few thoughts about your narrative:

- Your grief narrative should be no more than three pages.
- Begin by addressing your loved one, for example, Dear Dad.

- Remember: this is not a fact-finding mission but a narrative, a story, a letter to a loved one. Don't get bogged down in facts; instead, focus on the heart and spirit of the relationship.

- Include these components:

   1. How did your loved one make you laugh and how did they love you? What were the most important lessons they taught you?

   2. What do you need to apologize for? What are those unsaid things you never got to say that you think are vital? Do you have any regrets about this relationship? Make sure you've forgiven yourself of these.

   3. What do you wish they had done differently? Recount the sins, hurts, and emotions that have negatively touched you and that you never resolved with them. Have you extended forgiveness to them? Even though they are no longer with you, forgiveness may still be in order. This section may be the most difficult part of your loss.

   4. Include a noteworthy statement of what you miss most about your loved one. This was a very challenging part of the letter for me.

   5. Say goodbye to the hurts in the relationship *but not* to the relationship. Chapter 8 discusses the enduring relationships we can still enjoy with our departed loved ones.

Use the Rough Draft on pages 100-102 to make notes before actually writing out your letter. You can then use pages 103-105 to write your letter.

Set aside a special time to complete this assignment. This is really important. It may be a difficult task, but one that will pay great dividends going forward. Ask your spouse or roommates for space (and grace) this week, as it may be an emotional time for you.

Next week, in the *Grief Journey* group, pair up to read your letter to a partner. Each of you will have time to read your letters—this should take about 10 minutes each—and then you will change roles. After you both read your letters, reconvene with the group and share your experience.

Below are a few reminders that will prove helpful.

Storyteller: Read your letter. Take time to pause or cry if needed—this is your time.

Listener: Do not interrupt with questions, comments, or touching, but simply listen. You may cry, smile, or laugh (if appropriate) but do not touch or respond to the storyteller's letter. Do your very best to stay "present" with the storyteller, taking in the essence of the letter you are hearing. After one partner reads his or her letter, roles can be reversed.

ROUGH DRAFT – PAGE 1

_____

_____

_____

_____

_____

_____

_____

_____

_____

_____

_____

_____

_____

_____

_____

_____

_____

_____

_____

_____

_____

_____

_____

_____

_____

_____

_____

_____

ROUGH DRAFT – PAGE 2

_____

_____

_____

_____

_____

_____

_____

_____

_____

_____

_____

_____

_____

_____

_____

_____

_____

_____

_____

_____

_____

_____

_____

_____

_____

_____

_____

ROUGH DRAFT – PAGE 3

_____

_____

_____

_____

_____

_____

_____

_____

_____

_____

_____

_____

_____

_____

_____

_____

_____

_____

_____

_____

_____

_____

_____

_____

_____

LETTER TO MY LOVED ONE – PAGE 1

_____

_____

_____

_____

_____

_____

_____

_____

_____

_____

_____

_____

_____

_____

_____

_____

_____

_____

_____

_____

_____

_____

_____

_____

_____

LETTER TO MY LOVED ONE – PAGE 2

_____

_____

_____

_____

_____

_____

_____

_____

_____

_____

_____

_____

_____

_____

_____

_____

_____

_____

_____

_____

_____

_____

_____

_____

LETTER TO MY LOVED ONE – PAGE 3

_____

_____

_____

_____

_____

_____

_____

_____

_____

_____

_____

_____

_____

_____

_____

_____

_____

_____

_____

_____

_____

_____

_____

_____

Digging Deeper

My greatest fear in writing this letter was: _____

_____

_____

_____

_____

_____

After writing my letter I realize the following insights: _____

_____

_____

_____

_____

_____

More thoughts: _____

_____

_____

_____

_____

_____

_____

_____

JOURNALING

JOURNALING

_____

_____

_____

_____

_____

_____

_____

_____

_____

_____

_____

_____

_____

_____

_____

_____

_____

_____

_____

_____

_____

_____

_____

_____

_____

_____

JOURNALING

_____

_____

_____

_____

_____

_____

_____

_____

_____

_____

_____

_____

_____

_____

_____

_____

_____

_____

_____

_____

_____

_____

_____

CHAPTER EIGHT

ENDURING RELATIONSHIPS: FINDING SOLACE & JOY

You live in the hearts of everyone you've touched and nurtured while you were here. Death ends a life, not a relationship. — Mitch Albom, *Tuesdays with Morrie*

I was feeling some serious frustration as I was writing my dissertation for my Ph.D. I was diving into an area (writing) I had no experience in. In the final year of my doctorate studies, I was thinking more and more like quitting. It had been a good ride—informative, exciting at times, and helped with a salary increase at my job. But to write an entire research-based book? Perhaps I had reached my limit.

I stood up from my desk and walked into our "piano room," which has an antique piano with my mom's picture and her ashes in a small urn—and I began to share with her my frustrations. Not one to spend much time talking to the dead, I found myself pouring out my insecurities, doubts, and fears of my research writing to my mom.

As I did this, her "voice" came back to me—not an audible voice but her voice all the same. Those words of affirmation, "Tim, you absolutely can do this, be patient, quit your complaining, and get back to work!" The 50-plus years of hearing her voice, her patience with me, her unequivocal intensity about education, and her absolute positive outlook on life reverberated in my soul.

I left the room determined to get back to my dissertation writing. Within a year, I finished my writing and successfully defended it. I get emotional thinking about this.

We have an enduring relationship with our loved ones—an ongoing history—how can we not? Our loved ones influenced us in a multitude of ways. Many decisions we currently make are influenced by that history.

Instead of using words like acceptance, closure and guilt, we find different ways to frame our grief journey and our enduring relationship with our loved one. We are better served on our grief journey by words like honor, love, remembrance, and reminiscence. Ideas like imitation, history, and connection hold so much more hope and honor as we continue this voyage called life.

The great Apostle Paul, as he urged the newly formed churches to get stronger, constantly brought them back to their roots in the Old Testament.

He urged them by reminding them of the saints of old, the heroes in the faith, and the amazing ways God worked in their ancestors' lives to bring history up to Paul's time. Paul said it like this:

> *For everything that was written in the past was written to teach us, so that through the endurance taught in the Scriptures and the encouragement they provide we might have hope.* —Romans 15:4

Paul said the entire Old Testament was written to teach us, train us, and remind us that God is always working in relationships to make us stronger. The strength that we find from drawing upon our ancestors' faith gives us hope to continue to grow. You either made a decision, are making a decision at a specific moment in time, or will make a decision in the future.

In Hebrews 12:1, the writer reminds us that we are "surrounded by a great cloud of witnesses." As we live our lives, we find ourselves surrounded by the men and women of old, urging us on. Words like finality and acceptance, found in traditional grief research, don't seem to capture this spirit. Instead, consider God's perspective on relationships.

GOD'S PERSPECTIVE OF RELATIONSHIPS THROUGH THE AGES

History and memories can be a static set of facts and dates or they can be living experiences that give us hope. We've been given these past experiences—narratives we carry within—that have an impact on how we think and feel and who we will be in life.

We find hope that in some ways the life of our loved one continues on with us. They live on, within us, in the daily decisions we make, our current relationships and, in our hearts to remember them and honor them by keeping their memory current. They remain a living, vital part of us each today.

STONES

God uses stones to remind us of his heart for us through the lives of our ancestors, and the powerful dynamics of our relationships with those who have gone before us. Stones, rocks, minerals, and ancient carbon materials that have been in the earth for a millennium.

Stones remind us of many dynamic features of God's handiwork among us.

Stones used to kill giants and God's enemies. Stones were used to lay foundations for buildings or walls, precious stones were given as gifts or used in crowns. And then of course, Jesus, the greatest of all stones, became the chief cornerstone of every Christian's faith.

God also used memorial stones to remind the Israelites of the rich, textured, and expansive history of their forebears, not just for that generation but for all generations. Consider the nation of Israel in the book of Joshua.

> *So Joshua called together the twelve men he had appointed from the Israelites, one from each tribe, and said to them, "Go over before the ark of the Lord your God into the middle of the Jordan. Each of you is to take up a stone on his shoulder, according to the number of the tribes of the Israelites, to serve as a sign among you. In the future, when your children ask you, 'What do these stones mean?' tell them that the flow of the Jordan was cut off before the ark of the covenant of the Lord. When it crossed the Jordan, the waters of the Jordan were cut off. These stones are to be a memorial to the people of Israel forever.* —Joshua 4:4-7

Joshua called his leaders to carry stones to remind them of God's work in their lives from ages past and to serve as a sign. A sign of what? A sign of God's great works in the lives of his people. A sign for future generations to remember how their ancestors had lived their lives and to remember and apply the lessons their ancestors had been taught by God. For one generation only? No, forever.

Let's peer into the mind of God as he looks into the future of His people. As God considered leading his people, he used men and women and their experiences to "pay it forward" to the future generations. **In other words, we are to reach back in history to influence our current walk.** The acts, faith, love, and teachings of our forebears are present in current events for us. They influence the decisions we make today and tomorrow. And our decisions have the power to influence future generations.

In Exodus, God commands his people to carefully make decisions. How does he do this? He called them to make very elaborate and beautiful garments, adorned with stones. The stones on the ephod (an ornate jacket worn by priests) were a remembrance of those who had gone before, as the living approached God to make decisions. priests).

Memorials are an integral part of our human existence. Humans are constantly drawing upon their history to live life today. Washington, D.C., is full of legendary memorials we cherish as a nation and draw inspiration from. Some go to school for years to become archeologists to dig up the past. Museums are built to house precious, centuries-old documents that we still use to lead our system of government. Christians take communion (a memorial) every Sunday at church to remember Jesus. Memorials matter.

Even in our homes we have memorials, such as pictures, scrapbooks, keepsakes, and other artifacts that recall a rich family history of meaning. As my parents' home went up for auction, I brought home a carful of paintings, furniture, and knickknacks from their home to my house in Denver. My wife, Jackie, did a remarkable job of "integrating" these possessions into our home as a constant reminder of my parents' influence in my life. I am writing this book sitting at my mother's writing desk—a desk that is symbolic of her academic influence in my life.

We create memorials that are not simply static artifacts and materials but memorials that help us to make decisions. These memorials allow us to harken back to times, lessons, advice, acts of heroism, and courage from our ancestors that influence and challenge our lives. Memorials are there to change us, to make us better people, who hopefully are able to pass on wisdom, courage, lessons, and advice to another generation.

Memories are one facet of God's intention in our relationships with those no longer with us. Another is honoring our ancestors by the decisions we make. As the priests entered into the temple to enact God's decisions for His people, God called them to wear these stones as a memorial over their hearts. What a colorful and marvelous illustration of our enduring relationships.

Consider what Moses wrote:

> *Make the ephod of gold, and of blue, purple and scarlet yarn, and of finely twisted linen—the work of skilled hands. It is to have two shoulder pieces attached to two of its corners, so it can be fastened. Its skillfully woven*

> *waistband is to be like it—of one piece with the ephod and made with gold, and with blue, purple and scarlet yarn, and with finely twisted linen. Take two onyx stones and engrave on them the names of the sons of Israel in the order of their birth—six names on one stone and the remaining six on the other. Engrave the names of the sons of Israel on the two stones the way a gem cutter engraves a seal. Then mount the stones in gold filigree settings and fasten them on the shoulder pieces of the ephod as memorial stones for the sons of Israel. Aaron is to bear the names on his shoulders as a memorial before the Lord.* —Exodus 28:6-12

I find this remarkable, that I am part of a long line of decision makers, who have impacted my life, and now I have the opportunity to do the same for those who come after me.

In the same way the 12 sons of Israel bring meaning to God's people in Exodus 28, our ancestors bring meaning to us. The lives they lived, what they did, whether good or bad, are still important in our decision making today.

We can't deny the impact our loved ones still have on our lives. I can't make a decision (consciously or unconsciously) without taking into account my parents' values, especially when a decision involves my heart. Their imprint on me is indelibly intertwined with my way of thinking, my emotional makeup, my personality, and in many other ways. I am a product of their lives.

Not only does this apply to the past but the future. If my deceased loved ones have this influence on me, I, too, will have influence on my loved ones after I'm gone. This has huge implications on how I live my life now. Peter reminds us that we are living stones, who follow Jesus, the living stone.

> *As you come to him, the living Stone—rejected by humans but chosen by God and precious to him— you also, like living stones, are being built into a spiritual house to be a holy priesthood, offering spiritual sacrifices acceptable to God through Jesus Christ.* —1 Peter 2:4-5

As living stones, we live our lives by loving God and trying our best to love our families, friends, the church, our neighbors, and others. We draw on the work, love, and faith of our loved ones, their influence in our lives–all which influences how we live.

In fact, I am deeply influenced not only by my parents but also by my grandparents and others who impacted the lives of my mom and dad. Virtually every decision, act of love, thought and action, in some ways harkens back to their influence in my life. I find this personal thread through time to be inspiring, exciting, encouraging, and comforting.

We all want to be remembered. By honoring our loved ones, we lend perspective to our lives and places in history and give credence to James 4:14:

Why, you do not even know what will happen tomorrow. What is your life? You are a mist that appears for a little while and then vanishes.

LIVING STONES & ENDURING RELATIONSHIPS

In *Tuesdays with Morrie*, Morrie Schwartz wrote, "You live in the hearts of everyone you've touched and nurtured while you were here. Death ends a life but not a relationship." While we can no longer carry on with a physical relationship with our loved one, we carry on many aspects of the relationship by the decisions we make, in particular, the decisions of our hearts.

We can choose to not only remember our loved ones, but we can honor them by living out their values, lessons, and love in our lives. In every decision we make, every act of love, we bring along our loved one's influence.

My mother and father's values, ideals, thoughts, and experiences live on in my values, ideals, thoughts, and experiences. I choose to give them credit for much of my education, my choice of a wife, how I raised our kids, and so much more. I find this quite motivating and meaningful. I also think it is impossible to separate these.

Instead of words like closure, forgetting, or acceptance, incorporate concepts such as connections, continued relationship, remembering, and honoring into your griever's vocabulary. Work on honoring, linking, and connecting—not severing ties—with our loved ones.

An "enduring relationship" approach that focuses on remembering lives in contrast to forgetting is comforting, life-enhancing, and sustainable. Such an approach to life does not dwell on the pain of loss and is more than wistful reminiscing; it honors to a greater degree your relationship with your loved one.

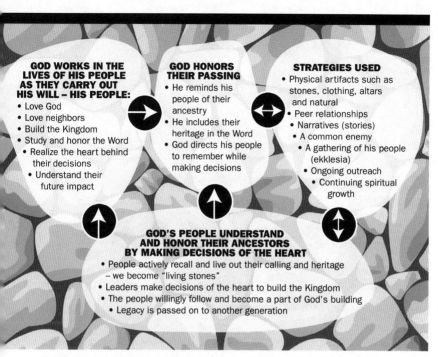

FIGURE 1 – LIVING STONES: HOW TO HONOR YOUR LOVED ONES

MEMORIALS, ALTARS AND RITUALS

Dad died at 7:00 a.m. on Jan. 1, 2011 in his home. As we gathered around his body and the tears began to subside, the stories came. My brother Danny said, "Wait a minute, this occasion calls for a rum & coke" (my Dad's favorite drink). So there at 8:30 a.m. on New Year's Day, we each poured a rum & coke and told stories about our dad—a memory I'll always cherish.

Now every January 1st—in our different cities—we all pour a rum & coke, tell stories about Dad and then post pictures on Facebook. It has become a unique ritual that honors our dad and brings us joy. I'm smiling as I write this.

Another ritual I have is to honor my mom every February 20th (the day she died) by imitating one of her fine qualities. One year I decided to go snow skiing at the Loveland ski area to the Bowls (these are "double X" expert runs, which I had no business being on) by myself in her honor. I wanted to spend the day thinking about her and her adventurous spirit.

Unfortunately, I took it a step too far. After many fruitless attempts at getting down the hill (each attempt resulting me face-planted in the snow), I finally gave up and stomped my way back down the hill sans skis. Instead of honoring her adventurous spirit, I imitated her wonderful sense of humor, having a good laugh at myself!

What about you? In what ways can you carry on the memory and honor your loved one in meaningful ways? Here are a few ideas on how to honor those we've lost:

- Journal your thoughts in a special book.

- Look at pictures of the good times or create a scrapbook.

- Watch a movie that reminds you of your loved one.

- Read a book that exemplifies the character of your loved one.

- Build a memorial in your home by placing a picture of your loved one, perhaps their favorite book or an urn with their ashes on a bookshelf.

- Occasionally take time to reflect and consider the "voice" of your loved one.

- I occasionally wear my dad's jacket to work and spend time thinking about him in a special way for the day.

- Create unique family traditions.

> **"Work on honoring, linking and connecting, not severing ties with our loved ones!"**

Digging Deeper

Ideas to honor my loved one:

- Memorial –

- Pictures –

- Special artifacts –

- Special dates –

- Rituals –

- Activities –

What values do I most appreciate about my loved one, and how do I see myself illustrating their values in my life?" _____

_____

_____

_____

_____

_____

How do I see my loved one in the way I make decisions? _____

_____

_____

_____

_____

_____

What do I want to be remembered for? _____

_____

_____

_____

_____

_____

How will I continue to receive support in this journey? _____

_____

_____

_____

_____

Who will I talk to if something comes up that is difficult? _____

_____

_____

Jot down any unanswered questions you still have about grief and loss and
commit to yourself to get them answered. _____

_____

_____

_____

_____

_____

_____

JOURNALING

JOURNALING

JOURNALING

EPILOGUE

WHERE DO WE GO FROM HERE?

The morning of February 20, 2007, the day my mom passed, marked for me an important turn in my journey of grief. Not only did it begin my grief journey, but it also marked an important shift in my grief paradigm. No longer wanting to ignore my grief, I took the day off of work and decided to attend my ethnography class later that evening. I could have missed the class and had a good excuse to do so, but something in me said I should go to honor my mom and what she meant to me. It was not an easy drive north, but one that I needed to do to begin an honoring tribute to her.

Many decisions I make, some intentionally and some unconsciously, harken back to my parents. I've come to realize that they still live in me, a fact, that sometimes brings on new lessons in grief. That's fine. Queen

Elizabeth II said it this way, "Grief is the price we pay for love." For me, my grief simply demonstrates my love for my parents and the respect they deserve for all the love they gave me.

You've learned that engaging grief like Jesus is not only vital to living well, but also necessary for honoring those you've lost. Experiencing the Father as he draws near to us in our grief proves comforting and sometimes unexpectedly reassuring. Taking our grief social (mourning) is essential to moving forward. Learning about our lifetime of loss and how we deal with grief has given us insight and tools for the future. The difficult task of writing our narrative and saying goodbye to hurts clears the way to having an enduring relationship with our loved ones. We've come to understand that memorials are living and potentially life changing.

And yet, life remains uncertain. Grief may linger. Losses will continue to mount and we will probably struggle at times. There will be times the loss still hurts and this challenge may present itself in new and unique ways.

Hopefully, this book has allowed you the time, space, knowledge, and support in your grief journey, and you are better equipped to navigate the sometimes-turbulent waters of grief.

Here are a few suggestions for those times when grief revisits us:

1.   Review your notes from *Grief Journey*. These concepts are timeless and will be a help to you. Often, we simply need reminders to deal with current challenges. Perhaps new insights will be added to your journal.

2.   Are you honoring your loved one in unique and special ways? Remember anniversaries, birthdays, and special events. Consider creating a memorial if you've not done so yet.

3.   Stay in touch with group members. You've probably created a special bond with someone in the group and chances are they may need your help as well.

4.   Consider a topical study from the Scriptures on God's comfort, compassion, and care for His people. Reading a different book on grief recovery may prove useful.

5.   If you find yourself experiencing severe difficulties after implementing these suggestions, consider seeking out a professional counselor.

6.   See Resources on page 129 for ideas.

THANK YOU MY FELLOW SOJOURNER

I want to thank you for reading this book and my story. It is comforting to me to know that my journey is not one I take alone but with other sojourners like you. Our God is a good God and he loves us dearly. He will continue to heal your broken heart as you eagerly seek him out. *Soli Deo Gloria!*

A few years back I was visiting my kids in China, where they both served in a mission church and teach English. While there I spoke with a college student, Oscar, who was busy studying the Bible as he looked into becoming a Christian. He asked in broken English (I listened in my nonexistent Mandarin Chinese), "Why do you believe the Bible is from God?"

I could have answered in many different ways but wanted to keep things simple. My answer to Oscar was this: I believe the Bible because in it I read about Jesus and the *multitude of ways that he loved people*, and that causes me to believe. I continue to seek him out, study his astonishing words, enjoy his incredible love, and take comfort in his undying friendship with me and I will never walk away from him. Oscar was baptized later that week.

Jesus is my hero, mentor, my Lord and Savior, and my friend. I continue to seek him out, study his amazing words, his incredible love, and his undying friendship with me. May we always walk with Him on our journey of grief.

Please feel free to email me with any questions or suggestions you may have at timothysumerlin@gmail.com.

GRIEF JOURNEY RESOURCES »

SUGGESTED BOOKS

- *The Grief Recovery Handbook 20th Anniversary Expanded Edition: The Action Program for Moving Beyond Death, Divorce, and Other Losses including Health, Career, and Faith*, Russell Friedman & John James

- *An Autumn's Journey: Deep Growth in the Grief and Loss of Life's Seasons*, Craig Lounsbrough

- *Healing After Loss: Daily Meditations for Working Through Grief*, Martha Hickman

- *Understanding Your Grief: Ten Essential Touchstones for Finding Hope and Healing Your Heart*, Dr. Alan Wolfelt

- *A Grief Observed (Collected Letters of C.S. Lewis)*, C.S. Lewis

- *Gone From My Sight: The Dying Experience*, Barbara Karnes, RN

- *Final Gifts: Understanding the Special Awareness, Needs, and Communications of the Dying*, Maggie Callanan

NATIONWIDE GROUPS AND RESOURCES

- GriefShare—free daily emails and information for local support groups. (www.griefshare.com).

- For help in finding an effective Christian counselor, read this article from CCEF.org:

  http://www.ccef.org/counseling/choosing-a-christian-counselor.

- Focus on the Family:

  http://www.focusonthefamily.com/lifechallenges/emotional-health/coping-with-death-and-grief/understanding-the-grieving-process.

- Online Grief Support—A Social Community: www.onlinegriefsupport.com.

- From the Stephen's Ministry—*Journeying Through Grief:* These four booklets are timed to arrive at crucial times in the grief journey and are only $10 a set. Consider them for yourself or a friend. www.stephenministries.org.

APPENDIX A
HELPING THE HURTING FRIEND

Often, we struggle with how to help the griever—what to say, what not to say, how to act, and how to love. For those helpers and friends, a few thoughts:

Timing. Often, when a death occurs there is an outpouring of support. Neighbors and friends bring meals, relatives fly in from out of state, and cards usually pour in. The details of planning the funeral and time spent with family often keep us occupied and "dealing" with our grief. But the weeks after the funeral may be the toughest part for many of us. As the loneliness sets in, the reality that we will now live without our loved one greets us every day and extreme emotional swings may suddenly appear.

Keep an eye on those who are three or so weeks past the funeral. This is often a crucial time for the griever and an opportunity to meet important needs. I often wait until this time to reach out to those I am not the main support for. I will often send a card and then reach out with a meal or initiate some time for coffee. Do not be offended if your grieving friend is not ready to talk. Be patient and offer help at another time. Allow your friend to direct such help if appropriate or offer ways to support.

Create a safe and confidential environment. Generally, the griever wants to talk, but careful planning and foresight are essential. A helping conversation is not the kind of discussion that is accomplished in a few minutes of fellowship or in passing. Ask your friend out for coffee or to a place that is conducive to this kind of conversation. Allocate at least an hour or so and be ready for more time if needed. Decide beforehand to be a listener and not a talker. Seek advice from a more seasoned mentor on how to help.

Listen and learn. This may be the most important and helpful feature of helping those who are grieving. Listening in a nonjudgmental fashion will allow your friend to open up in a safe and confidential manner. Listening with empathy, that is, going into your own painful experiences to feel what they might be feeling is critical. This doesn't mean you are trying to relate to their specific experience, but you feel similar hurts and are able to connect emotionally.

This kind of attentive listening takes great humility and will allow you to stay present in their pain. Refuse the temptation to listen and fix. There is no "fixing" grief—just staying in the moment and conveying love. Acknowledge the pain, stay with it, and simply love. Be willing to hear the same story repeatedly —it may be cathartic to your friend. Always use sensitivity, appropriate touch, warmth, and good eye contact.

Pray for a heart that offers hope. This is not easy work. As friends, we must have faithful hearts that believe in a God of compassion who comforts and offers relief. This can be tricky. You don't want to offer platitudes and pat answers that belittle someone's pain. At the same time, we want to comfort with God's Word at appropriate times. Pray before you meet with your friend and ask God for wisdom and insight. Have a scripture ready or leave a card with comforting thoughts.

Asking questions that spur good conversation. Timely questions are essential for a conversation to move in a positive direction. Typically, trying to relate to a friend's grief is not useful at this time. Work on keeping your friend talking. Questions that keep the conversation moving are:

- Tell me about your loved one.
- What do you miss the most about them?
- What has been the most difficult thing for you?
- What has helped you the most so far?

This may require some practice and patience. Allow silence to be OK. Remember to "Hold the Moment" from Chapter 1. Allowing the space to think and feel is important.

Love and act. Developing a faith that allows for action while a friend is-grieving and in confusion, demonstrates love and concern that will make a huge difference. Finding ways to serve in the midst of a friend's grief not only eases their pain but also communicates love.

This statement is not helpful: "If I can help let me know." This puts the burden back on the griever and can come across as not caring. Instead, say "I know you need the lawn mowed this week, I'll come over on Thursday." Or perhaps initiate a project together.

Many grievers want to find some normalcy in life and a simple activity with you will demonstrate that life carries on. At times your friend may simply want to do a "non-grief" activity like a movie. Be perceptive to these opportunities.

Remember. One of the most difficult areas of grief is the way life may cause us to forget our loved one. Our loved ones want to be remembered too. Try to initiate a conversation a few weeks out from someone's loss of a loved one. I often put in my Google calendar the date of the passing of a friend's loved one and send an email, card or make a phone call on the anniversary of the death.

*Review Chapter Three—We Reach Out: Our Friends, Family and Grief.

APPENDIX B
WHY GRIEF RECOVERY SHOULD BE AN INTEGRAL PART OF THE CHURCH[1]

There has been a trending in the past decade in many churches away from counseling in the church, toward private therapy—that is, Christians going outside the church for their grief counseling needs.

While private counseling may be both appropriate and warranted, it has become at times, both ineffective and expensive. Ephesians 3 and 4 make it abundantly clear that we are to counsel one another in the church and, we have powerful and effective resources (small groups, house churches, counselor-trained Christians) to do so. Consider the following passage from the book of Ephesians as Paul described one of the functions of the church:

1. Makes plain the gospel message.

> *Although I am less than the least of all the Lord's people, this grace was given me: to preach to the Gentiles the boundless riches of Christ, and to make plain to everyone the administration of this mystery, which for ages past was kept hidden in God, who created all things. His intent was that now, through the church, the manifold wisdom of God should be made known to the rulers and authorities in the heavenly realms, according to his eternal purpose that he accomplished in Christ Jesus our Lord. In him and through faith in him we may approach God with freedom and confidence.*
> —Ephesians 3:8-12

Some believers may not need much help in understanding God's unending grace, found in the gospel message, in their lives during times of grief. Many though, because of complex grief issues, a history of abuse, addictive behavior, mental health challenges, or the consequences of sin, need help in **understanding and applying the gospel message in their lives during their grief journey.** As leaders and fellow sojourners, we are called to make the gospel **plain, understandable and relevant.**

Christians are not defined as "problems" or "clients" but are identified within the church, as people with gifts and specific talents. We are all given a greater role to play in the church that exceeds any grief issues we may have. Hearts can (and should be) revealed, counseled, and attended to in the church setting.

2. Reveals and implements the power of God.

I pray that out of his glorious riches he may strengthen you with power through his Spirit in your inner being, so that Christ may dwell in your hearts through faith. And I pray that you, being rooted and established in love, may have power, together with all the Lord's holy people, to grasp how wide and long and high and deep is the love of Christ, and to know this love that surpasses knowledge—that you may be filled to the measure of all the fullness of God. Now to him who is able to do immeasurably more than all we ask or imagine, according to his power that is at work within us, to him be glory in the church and in Christ Jesus throughout all generations, for ever and ever! Amen. —Ephesians 3:16-21

Accessing the Holy Spirit's power to travel the journey of grief at times may elude the grieving Christian. But having mature and caring group leaders and members to guide and access God's available power is essential. Small group leaders, pastors, ministers, deacons, counselor-trained Christians, and elders know personal back stories and the unique challenges of being a Christian unlike the office-bound professional counselor.

We know the direction of the church, the sermons taught, the specific problems a church may face, and the history of the grieving believer. Rather than a "designated expert" and a "needy client," the body of Christ works in unique and Christ-centered ways. The richness of the church setting rises above the office-bound counselor in effectiveness and opportunity to give glory to God. Mourning (grief expressed publicly) is best demonstrated in the church setting.

3. Prepares God's people for works of service.

So Christ himself gave the apostles, the prophets, the evangelists, the pastors and teachers, to prepare his people for works of service, so that the body of Christ may be built up until we all reach unity in the faith and in the knowledge of the Son of God and become mature, attaining to the whole measure of the fullness of Christ. Then we will no longer be infants, tossed back and forth by the waves, and blown here and there by every wind of teaching and by the cunning and craftiness of people in their deceitful scheming. Instead, speaking the truth in love, we will grow to become in every respect the mature body of him who is the head, that is, Christ. From him the whole body, joined and held together by every supporting ligament, grows and builds itself up in love, as each part does its work. —Ephesians 4:11-16

Each part doing its work—every member in your church can be working and living to their full potential! The grieving Christian has the ability and opportunity to be completely open about the personal workings of God's Spirit, the challenges of outreach, the life of worship, the significance of Scripture, and the social dynamics of their participation in the church during times of grief. Christians who experience the full journey of grief serve in powerful ways—many for the first time in years. Also, the most important questions can be addressed. What is my purpose? How do I identify myself? The church is a safe, and confidential environment to answer these and other essential questions.

END NOTE

[1] This article was influenced by the work of the Christian Counseling Educational Foundation's work on counseling in the local church (ccef.org). CCEF is the best Christian counseling group I know of. They are led by David Powlison, Ed Welch and Mike Emlet, among others. They also create and publish the "Journal of Biblical Counseling."

If you are interested in learning more about beginning a counseling ministry in your church, visit inmotioncounseling.org or email Tim at timothysumerlin@gmail.com.

APPENDIX C
UNIQUE CHALLENGES OF SUICIDE

But you, Lord, are a compassionate and gracious God, slow to anger,
abounding in love and faithfulness. —Psalm 86:15

Suicide is one of the leading causes of death in America and around the world. It afflicts the young and old. I've had to deal with this for 30 years as a counselor – dear friends and students who have completed suicide. My role as a counselor is usually twofold: I teach about suicide prevention, and I counsel those closest to individuals who have taken their lives, and help them cope with the emotional disarray afterwards. I've rarely focused on the in-between—the work of compassion. That all changed when close friends and long-time members of the Denver Church of Christ, lost their son, Nick, to suicide.

The church was packed for Nick's funeral, and the mood was somber, supportive, and loving, as the church gathered to comfort Nick's family. Nick became a Christian as a teen and was a wonderful young man, who enjoyed serving, and making others laugh. Unfortunately, he also had a mental health diagnosis that robbed him of his innocence and youth. He was a shadow of the fun-loving kid, we once knew. His parents and siblings did all they could to help, including attending mental health seminars, getting advice, and wrapping their loving arms around their son. But it wasn't enough.

Facing loss is never easy and suicide in particular. How do you talk about this? Most don't or they simply skirt the issue with euphemisms. We use words like, "untimely" and "unexpected death" to describe suicide but find it difficult to discuss the topic openly. By avoiding the issue, we leave it in the shadows.

Often, we get judgmental toward those closest to the deceased. If we don't say it, we feel it or think it: "What was the matter with the family?" "How could they miss this?" "Suicide is the most selfish thing a person can do." Some actually say these words—I have. Until this young man's memorial service woke me up.

Our senior minister, John Lusk[2] shared a thoughtful and empathetic message on how God looks at suicide and how we need to respond. This is an excerpt from the devotional taught that day by John.

GOD, THE FATHER OF COMPASSION

The Bible has something to say about compassion. God is the Father of Compassion—it is in his very DNA. He created compassion, sustains it and wants his people to practice it. Consider the following Scriptures:

Praise be to the God and Father of our Lord Jesus Christ, the Father of compassion and the God of all comfort —2 Corinthians 1:3

The Lord is good to all; he has compassion on all he has made. —Psalm 145:9

God is the Father of Compassion. He invented it, constructed it and lives it. Compassion resides in God. All through the Scriptures, God breathes, lives, demonstrates and emulates compassion. Compassion is not simply a characteristic of God – *it is in his very DNA as who He is.*

God Demonstrates Compassion Through All of Life—the Good, the Bad, the Ugly.

But the Lord was gracious to them and had compassion and showed concern for them because of his covenant with Abraham, Isaac and Jacob. To this day he has been unwilling to destroy them or banish them from his presence. —2 Kings 13:23

Can a mother forget the baby at her breast and have no compassion on the child she has borne? Though she may forget, I will not forget you! —Isaiah 49:15

God made a promise of compassion to his people. He cannot go back on his promises and will show compassion throughout our lives.

Compassion That Shows Mercy in our Sin.

Have mercy on me, O God, according to your unfailing love; according to your great compassion blot out my transgressions. —Psalm 51:1

Because of the Lord's great love we are not consumed, for his compassions never fail. —Lamentations 3:22

So he got up and went to his father. But while he was still a long way off, his father saw him and was filled with compassion for him; he ran to his son, threw his arms around him and kissed him. —Luke 15:20

God shows compassion while we are at our worst. His compassion is not always dependent on our behavior, but as our Father, he shows compassion when we need it most. *What sins have you committed that God has not had compassion on?*

His compassion and mercy is the very character of God that compels us to change and serve him—it's that powerful! Now, we can be compassionate toward each other.

> *Be kind and compassionate to one another, forgiving each other,*
> *just as in Christ God forgave you.* —Ephesians 4:32

> *Therefore, as God's chosen people, holy and dearly loved, clothe yourselves with*
> *compassion, kindness, humility, gentleness and patience.* —Colossians 3:12

Since God is the father of compassion, we too should abound in compassion. As an imitator of God, we can follow his heart and show compassion on all. Let's park our judgmental spirit and show compassion. Allow God to judge, our role is one of compassion toward the family of the one who died and toward the one who completed the suicide.

> *—End of John's lesson (used with permission)*

Many complete suicide due to multifaceted mental health issues. Most authorities believe the complexities of mental health issues prevent us from adequately explaining why anyone would take their own life. Teenagers often lack the impulse control required to navigate through difficult developmental intricacies of their environment, and during complex times of challenge may turn to suicide.

This certainly does not mean we are ambivalent or apathetic towards those considering suicide or see it as a viable solution to life's challenges. The numbers who attended Nick's service was a testimony to the many people who cared for Nick and care for his family.

For those who contemplate such a fate, please get help. Find someone (an adult or professional) who can listen and help. Hope and help are always available.[3]

END NOTES

[1] Shared with permission of the Thompson family.

[2] John Lusk is the senior minister of the Denver Church of Christ and a big supporter of the Disciples In Motion ministry. If you'd like to hear him in person, check out his sermons at denverchurchofchrist.org."

[3] Resources: nimh.nih.gov, suicidepreventionlifeline.org and christiansuicideprevention.com."

APPENDIX D
LOSING A PET: IT MAY BE A BIGGER DEAL THAN YOU THINK!

In the middle of writing this book I had to put my beloved basset hound, Brewski, to sleep. He had put up with cancer for 18 long months and it was time to let go.

For eight years, I had hiked many miles of trails and camped out in the Colorado Rockies with Brewski. We had traveled twice to the East Coast from Denver to visit family (just the two of us). My kids adored him and he was so loved that my father had a portrait commissioned of him that sits above our fireplace. He even found a place in public devotionals for the Disciples In Motion[1] ministry. Almost 100 friends commented on my Facebook posting.

I had it all planned out, received plenty of advice, and made sure I had a reputable vet hospital to do the procedure. We spent a fantastic last day together—breakfast of sausage and eggs (for both of us), work in the garage together, three long walks, and a beer together on the back porch in honor of his name.

I felt ready to let go. We headed out to the veterinary hospital. This was the first time I had ever put a pet to sleep and I was unsure how it would go. It was not what I expected…

I had not taken into account the way Brewski had become an integral part of my life—even my identity. The following days were difficult. Some of the features I experienced grieving for my parents returned, such as rawness, doubts (about the timing of putting him to sleep), loneliness, sadness, and a feeling of emptiness (Brewski was no longer a fixture in my backyard).

Now, I don't want to overstate the loss of a pet and while most do not attend grief groups for pets, they do deserve some of our attention. Here are a few thoughts to consider as you grieve the loss of a pet:[2]

1) Pets love us unconditionally. We rarely have any bad memories of them—we miss their loyalty, comfort and friendliness. Brewski made my world more tolerable—he often made me laugh at life. He had no grudges, his tail was always wagging and he just wanted to be where I was. I miss his unconditional love for me.

2) We spend many hours with our pets. They live in our homes, "watch" the kids grow and, participate in many family activities. They indeed

become a part of the family! Their loss can create a new dynamic in the home and often a readjustment time may need to take place.

3) Pets can become a part of our identity. Brewski certainly did. When we went for walks or hiked on the trail, many stopped us and commented on him or wanted to pet him. He was my partner and made me look better! I enjoyed the way he helped me connect to others.

4) Others feel the loss of our pets. Pay attention to your children (this may be their first real loss) and spouse and be mindful of their individual needs during the loss. Facilitate good conversation around the loss and be willing to create an environment that allows for emotional responses.

5) Allow yourself time and space to grieve and mourn your pet. Try not to compare and minimalize your loss—just accept it for what it is. You can also adapt the exercises in this book to help you cope with the loss of your pet.

END NOTES

[1] For more information on the Disciples In Motion ministry go to www.inmotioncounseling.org.

[2] http://psychcentral.com/lib/grieving-the-loss-of-a-pet/

APPENDIX E
LEADING A GRIEF JOURNEY IN MOTION GROUP

Thank you for leading a *Grief Journey* group. Your compassionate leadership and alliance in this group will make a huge difference in many lives. Too many people walk alone on their grief journey, and this should not happen within the church.

Below you will find tips on leading this group, as well as a brief outline for each session. This appendix is not meant to be a substitute for training for leading the *Grief Journey* group. Group leaders should have some training in group leadership or counseling. If you desire training, inquire by email at timothysumerlin@gmail.com.

While this book (alone) may accommodate most any kind of grief, the *Grief Journey* group is best suited for those who have suffered the loss of a loved one, including miscarriages and abortions. Other issues that may be appropriate for the group setting are severe childhood abuse issues, divorce, terminal health issues, and other significant losses.

This is generally not an appropriate group for those who have lost pets, jobs, and relationships or have self-esteem issues. While these can be quite serious and need attention, I have found they may create a "disconnection" with other group members. Who to have in the group is your call—carefully consider the group dynamics.

A few items to consider as you set up a group:

- Advertise a few weeks in advance via normal church communication.

- Send emails to church leaders who may know of grief issues with their members.

- Consider planning the group for a time that is close to worship service. This is helpful as members are already at church and you'll improve attendance.

- It is crucial that the meeting room should provide a safe comfortable, and confidential setting.

- Group size is important—generally no smaller than six, no larger than 12.

- Remind members to read and journal in the "Introduction" and "Chapter One: Jesus Embraces Grief–Will You?" before the first group and to bring their books to group.

- It is best to have an even number of members (members pair up in the last three sessions); however, you, as the group leader, can be partnered with the "odd person out."

A few thoughts about leading the group time:

- It is essential to make these devotionals your own. Spend an ample amount of time learning the material and put sufficient care, compassion, and heart into it. Grievers are often in a fragile state, and they need a well-prepared devotional.

- Generally, the devotionals should last 20 to 25 minutes.

- Each week the entire group session should be about 75 to 90 minutes.

- Bring extra books, tissues, snacks, and bottles of water.

- Open and close groups with a prayer from a member.

WEEK ONE–INTRODUCTION & CHAPTER 1

*Hopefully members have already read and written in the journal in the "Introduction" and "Chapter One" before the group starts. Since this is the first week and some members may be getting their book at this session, suggest that they take notes as you go along.

Welcome the group and briefly share your own grief journey.

For about 10 minutes, share from the "Introduction" and the time and space concepts. At this point ask the group, "What are important group norms?" Make sure the following are discussed and emphasized:

- **No crosstalk or hugs during group.** This means no advising or "relating to" others as they share—simply allow members to say what they wish. This is an essential rule for the group. Often, when we "comfort" others as they are processing emotions, we stop the emotional journey God is allowing by interrupting, and we end up causing harm. After group is a great time to hug, comfort, and share words of encouragement. Remind them of the scripture: *Like one who takes away a garment on a cold day, or like vinegar poured on a wound, is one who sings songs to a heavy heart.* —Proverbs 25:20

- **No judgment regarding how to grieve.** Grief is a very unique journey and advising others on how, when, and what to grieve will possibly break trust, produce anger, and hurt, and indicate to other group members that it is not safe to share vulnerably.

- Make every effort to attend every meeting. Those who attend and fully participate are able to build confidence and trust as well as life-long friendships. When you miss a group, you miss important material, homework assignments and partnership times, which are essential later in the group session. Please let the group leader know if you have to miss a week.

- Stay focused on the journey of grief. This is not a time to discuss theologically sensitive topics (e.g., who is and who is not a Christian or other sensitive matters) but one of a lost relationship, the pain involved, and the vital work of healing a broken heart.

After a discussion of group rules, share the Chapter One devotional on Jesus engaging is grief. Make this lesson your own. Share it with care, compassion, and heart.

After the devotional time ask the following question:

1) Share your name, 2) why you are here, 3) what is one thing you would like the group to know about the person who died and 4) what is one thing you would like to get out of this experience?

After this time of discussion, close the group out:

- Explain the general course of how the next several weeks will proceed. Do this every week, as it will allow the members to have an idea of where they are headed.

- Discuss how to use the book—include the Digging Deeper sections (they provide personal application to the lesson) and the importance of journaling. *We get out of the group what we put in.*

- Most people spend at least an hour a week on their grief work. Members should have read and completed the work for the chapter before the group time.

- Collect email addresses. The group leader will email everyone during the week to review last week's lesson and let members know what is coming up next.

WEEK TWO – CHAPTER 2

Welcome and begin with a discussion:

- Does anyone have any questions from last week?

- Would anyone like to share something they learned from the reading or from group?

If there are new members, introduce them and have them share the last week's discussion question: Share your name, why you are here, one thing you would like the group to know about the person who died, and one thing you would like to get out of this experience.

After group sharing, lead the Chapter Two devotional on God's heart for the griever for about 20 minutes. Again, make this lesson your own and share with great care, heart, and compassion. Include a discussion question of your choice during this devotional. At the end of your devotional, ask:

What was it like when you heard about your loved one dying and how did you experience numbness?

This is usually a very difficult time of sharing but essential for group cohesion and personal reflection. Have tissues ready but allow for the uncomfortable times without other members interfering.

Close the group with a reminder about next week's lesson and a prayer. Email the group during the week.

WEEK THREE – CHAPTER 3

Welcome the group and ask:

- Does anyone have any questions from last week?
- Would anyone like to share something they learned from the reading or from group?

Introduce any new members and have them share: Share your name, why you are here, one thing you would like the group to know about the person who died, and one thing you would like to get out of this experience.

*This is the final week for new members.

Today's lesson will focus on our friends and family, and how they help or hurt us in our grief journey. We'll also discuss myths surrounding grief.

Conduct the Chapter Three devotional and after sharing about myths, ask:

- What are things others said or did to comfort you that did not help? What did these issues cause you to do?
- In light of the "four friends" can you think of a more helpful way others can help us in our grief journey?
- How has grieving helped you become closer to God and others?

We often have to direct the way our friends help us. (e.g. Would you listen for a while as I tell you what I miss most about my mom?)

Close out the group with a prayer and direction for next week. Email the group on Monday.

WEEK FOUR – CHAPTER 4

Welcome and begin with a discussion:

- Does anyone have any questions from last week?
- Would anyone like to share something they learned from the reading or from group?

Lead the devotional from Chapter 4.

After the devotional, ask the following questions:

- What kinds of themes did you see running through your response to the "Lifetime Loss Narrative?" Were there any surprises?
- How do you think you can change some of the negative responses you've seen?

Remind members of the assignment for next week.

WEEK FIVE – CHAPTER 5

Welcome and begin with a discussion:

- Does anyone have any questions from last week?
- Would anyone like to share something they learned from the reading or from group?

Lead the devotional from Chapter 5.

After the devotional, ask the following questions:

- What are some of the ways you've seen that you personally deal with your recent grief and the way it has impacted your life?
- What have you found effective in taking back control of the negative ways you've dealt with grief?

Remind members of the assignment for next week. We'll get together in pairs at the beginning of the group and share our thoughts from Chapter 6. Remember, this assignment is not a fact-finding mission but a narrative, a story.

WEEK SIX – CHAPTER 6

Welcome the group and ask:

- Does anyone have any questions from last week?
- Would anyone like to share something they learned from the reading or from group?

Lead Chapter Six devotional on examining a relationship. The goal of today is that you understand and communicate *the essence* of your relationship with your loved one. There will probably be both good and difficult things you share—be as honest as you possibly can. We will break into pairs (try to have spouses mix it up with someone other than their spouse). Explain the roles:

Storyteller: Share your story for up to 25 minutes. Remember, this is not a fact-finding mission but a story of the heart, try not to get bogged down in details, but stay with the essence of the story. Take time to pause or cry if needed—this is your time.

Listener: Please do not interrupt with questions, comments or touching, simply listen. You may cry, smile or laugh (if appropriate) but do not touch or respond to the storyteller's story. Do your very best to stay "present" with the storyteller, taking in the essence of the story you are hearing. Allow them ample time to pause or cry—this is their time.

- After 25 minutes change roles.
- After 50 or so minutes bring the group back together and ask:
- What was this experience like for you? What were the surprises?

Explain next week's assignment. You may consider having lunch for next week's group.

WEEK SEVEN – CHAPTER 7 AND 8

Welcome the group and ask:

- Does anyone have any questions from last week?
- Would anyone like to share something they learned from the reading or from group?

This is the final week. This week you will read your grief narrative in the same pairs you used last week. Remind the group of the following:

Emphasize that this is not saying goodbye to the relationship—only goodbye to hurts and unsaid things that hurt the relationship.

- We will break into pairs the same as last week—if a partner is not present the group leader will step in.

Storyteller: Read your letter. Take time to pause or cry if needed—this is your time.

Listener: Please do not interrupt with questions, comments or touching—simply listen. You may cry, smile or laugh (if appropriate) but do not touch or respond to the storyteller's letter. Do your very best to stay "present" with the reader, taking in the essence of the letter you are hearing. Allow them ample time to pause or cry—this is their time. After reading, you may hug and then change roles.

After 20 or so minutes bring the group back together and ask: What was this experience like for you? What were the surprises?

After this debrief time, lead the devotional found in Chapter 8. You may need to read this over a few times to get familiar with the material. After sharing the devotional, ask:

- How can you memorialize your loved one?

- What is it about enduring relationships that are helpful to you?

- What has helped you the most during the past six to eight weeks?

- How will you deal with any new issues that may arise?

Plan out the 'Epilogue Week.' This final meeting is usually done a few weeks after Week 7. This is a time to reconvene with members from the *Grief Journey* group; it is a time for fellowship, a meal together, to discuss how people at doing, and how to continue forward with their respective grief journeys.

WEEK EIGHT – EPILOGUE WEEK

Welcome the group and ask:

Consider having this meeting in a home of one of the members and sharing a potluck meal. Lead a short devotional to review the previous seven weeks and then lead a discussion using 3 or 4 of the following questions, as you deem appropriate:

- How have things gone since we last met?

- What are some of the challenges you are facing?

- What was the most helpful lesson for you in the past seven weeks?

- What are some ideas you have for support in the future?

APPENDIX F
GRIEF DREAMS

I was so moved by the dream I had about my mother—so much, that I prayed for a similar experience about my dad, and God answered my prayer.

In my dream, I was in my new office at my new job. Dad appeared with a mustache (something he rarely grew) and wearing his traditional blue sweater. We hugged and I asked him, "How are you?" He replied, "Fine." Dad was patient as I assembled his name on a refrigerator with magnetic letters. Just then, two students came to my door (I'm a school counselor) who I had to speak with. After the students left, my dad asked me to consider quitting my job to do something different, something more along my passions and that he would support me in doing so. The dream ended with my co-worker, Aaron, and I sitting outside of our offices, with me crying and trying to tell Aaron about the dream.

This dream was quite different from my mom's dream. It is more difficult to figure out and almost needs a Daniel-like figure to interpret it. For me, it was comforting just to see my dad, to remember his patience with me, the words of encouragement about a very pressing issue in my life, and my connection to my new friend and co-worker, Aaron.

Perhaps you've had dreams about your loved one. Hopefully, they were positive in nature. Not all are. Some dreams you may find troubling and best forgotten—you decide. If they were positive, hold on to them dearly and never forget them. I found it helpful to write them up the morning after and spend time pondering their meaning. As time marches on, grief dreams can take on new meanings than when they first made their debut. If nothing else, dreams about our loved ones are treasures to be cherished.

Take time to write your dream out. I put my dad's dream in my Google calendar on the date it happened, and review it every year. I try to give it meaning in my life. It is always a comfort for me and reassures me of my relationship with my dad.

The following is an excerpt from the book, *The Dream Messenger: How Dreams of the Departed Bring Healing Gifts* by Patricia Garfield. I found this information quite helpful as I considered my dreams—perhaps you will too:

Are these dream images of the dead simply memories of them, infused by our imagination, to help us cope with grief during bereavement? Are they part of an internal process we employ to adjust to loss and assist us in solving daily problems? Or are dream images of the dead actual encounters with the spirit of the deceased? Elisabeth Kübler-Ross thinks they are, calling dreams about the dead "true contacts on a spiritual plane."

There is no way yet known to prove either position: that dreams about the dead are "real" contacts; or that they are images conjured by the dreamer to meet psychological needs. Regardless of what may be the facts, we know that bereaved people dream about the lost person; that their dreams are exceptionally vivid and may dramatically alter the life and belief system of the dreamer.

Our relationship with the dead endures. In our dreams, the dead have messages for the living. The living also has messages for the dead that can be delivered in dreams. Conflicts left pending when the death occurred can sometimes find resolution in the meeting place of the dream.

Obviously, a person requires time to accomplish these tasks, but you will see how it is here that our dreams about the dead are especially helpful.

The Universal Dream About the Dead: I call the image of the deceased person the "dream." The composite dream I will describe depicts the common elements in the "journey of the dream messenger" that I found in hundreds of grief dreams. Not every dream about the dead contains all nine elements, but most dreams about the dead have several of them. In brief, they are: 1) the announcement, 2) the arrival, 3) the appearance, age, condition, and clothing of the dream messenger, 4) the attendants; 5) the message, 6) the gift, 7) the farewell embrace, 8) the departure and, 9) the aftermath. What follows is an ideal or complete model of a dream about the dead. This universal dream about the dead will help you understand your own dreams about them.

The dead live on in our dreams long after they die. We see them, yearn for them, talk with them, love them, fear them, hate them, or hold them. Sooner or later, you will have some of these dreams. Perhaps you have already.

Here's how it may transpire.

The Announcement

First of all, you are likely to sense that something unusual is coming. Dreamers describe feeling an anticipation, an odd awareness just prior to the signal predicting the imminent arrival of the dream messenger. The announcement that the dream messenger is here occurs in some way. By various signs and sensations, an announcement is made that the border between the living and the dead is about to be temporarily suspended. In a way, these dream images parallel what mythologist Joseph Campbell has labeled "the call to adventure." You—the hero or heroine of your dream—are about to have an adventure.

The Arrival at the Meeting Place

The announcement having been made, the dream messenger arrives in the dream. You may see the deceased. These transportation settings are places of transition that underscore the journey that is being undertaken by both the deceased and yourself. Often the place where the dreamer meets the dream messenger has some barrier between the living and the dead. It may be a simple garden gate; a barrier at the airport; a glass partition, or some other boundary marker. For a moment—through a door or a gate, in a hallway or a tunnel, in a room, a garden, a meadow, a station, or in outer space—the dreamer meets the dream messenger. You will find this element of a meeting place present in almost all of your dreams about the dead.

The Dream Messenger

Who is this dream messenger? The deceased, of course, but often the dead do not look exactly like themselves in dreams. Their appearance depends on your feelings—your hopes and your fears—about the dead person, and on the message that follows. Don't be surprised if the deceased has a different appearance.

Do they look ill or transfigured or positive? Do the dead look like themselves, or as you last saw them? These positive dream images of the dead make the dreamer very happy. They seem to convey a spirit at peace and give hope to the dreamer for a joyful afterlife.

The Attendants of the Dream Messenger

What is one to make of these "attendants"? Are they part of the "death party," as one might be part of a wedding party?

Look carefully at the dead, their facial expressions, their ages, conditions, and clothing—each aspect conveys clues to the messages they bring to you.

The Dream Message Delivered

Here we come to the heart of dreams about the dead. What messages do they bring the living, and in what form are they brought?

Negative Dream Messages: Turning to the contents of the message, I'll summarize here a few of the most frequent.

"I'm Suffering" Don't be startled if you experience some extremely unpleasant dreams about the dead at first. It is very common to see the deceased once again suffering the symptoms that caused death, either as they were in actuality, somewhat exaggerated, or grossly distorted. Especially if you were present at the death, or if the circumstances were sudden or violent, you are likely to "replay" the death scene. This type of nightmare is characteristic of the post-traumatic nightmares that follow violence or personal injury.sudden or violent, you are likely to "replay" the death scene. This type of nightmare is characteristic of the post-traumatic nightmares that follow violence or personal injury.

Positive Dream Messages

"I'm Not Really Dead." You may find yourself dumbfounded to see the person again, or just plain puzzled, as some dreamers were: I am astounded to see my dead uncle again, singing, laughing and making jokes; I say, "My God, what are you doing here? You're dead!" He smiles and replies, "Honey, when you die, you lose your body, not your sense of humor." The amount of humor in these dreams surprised me. It seemed to arise especially when it was typical of the deceased.

"I'm O.K.": By far, the most prevalent positive dream message you are likely to receive is "I'm O.K." In these dreams, you will meet the dead looking or acting as they did when young or healthy. This message is where the clothing of the dead is often flowing or shimmering, their hair glowing, their eyes sparkly, and faces bright. If the individual who died was a fetus or infant, the dream image will be a few years older, looking outstandingly well. This message has a number of variations in precise form, such as "Everything's all right," "I'm fine," "Don't worry about me," and so forth.

"Goodbye" Dreams: Another typical dream message you might get is "Goodbye." In this instance, you will see the dead person specifically take leave of you, saying in words, or by mental communication, "goodbye," "farewell." or "I have to leave now." Again, exact words may not be specified, but you will "know" during the dream or after you awaken that "so-and-so came to say goodbye to me."

These dreams often include physical contact, and the exchange of loving comments, as well as an affectionate goodbye. The dream message "Goodbye" is a classic. It has been reported over and over again in literature, usually when a death has taken place at a distance from the dreamer, or is sudden or vicious. You can also expect a "Goodbye" dream message to be delivered when you have been deprived of a chance to say goodbye in person.

Other positive dream messages include:

- "Here's a Gift"
- "Congratulations"
- "Stop!"
- "Go Ahead!"
- "Please Forgive Me"
- "I Forgive You"

- "I'm Evolving"   • "I'm Being Reborn"
- "I Give You Life"

Neutral Dream Messages: "Hi! How Are You?" As you enter the latter stages of bereavement, and perhaps sporadically throughout the remainder of your life, you may find yourself receiving a friendly visit from the dream messenger.

The Gift of the Dream Messenger

Most of these gifts represented love to the dreamer; one specifically symbolized artistic talent handed on from the deceased; another stood for forgiveness for the murder of the deceased. Gifts of love in words or images are especially comforting to the grieving dreamer. If you should dream of getting a present from a dead person, and it is something desirable to you, honor it. If its meaning is not clear at the moment, study the image. Find something in your waking life that is a reasonable facsimile and ponder it until its meaning for you emerges. These gifts from the dead can be precious beyond all riches. You may receive a unique dream message, especially designed for you.

The Farewell Embrace

A hug? Kiss? Handshake? A wave?

The Departure of the Dream Messenger

How did they leave the scene?

The Aftermath of the Visit

You may not only find yourself solaced by your dream about the dead, but also feel deeply loved. You may find inspiration and new confidence in the reality of an afterlife. Perhaps you, like so many before you, will find your life transformed by a visit from the dream messenger. Then the journey of the dream messenger is finished.

END NOTE

[1] Garfield, Patricia. *The Dream Messenger: How Dreams of the Departed Bring Healing Gifts,* Simon & Schuster, 1997.